Desperately Seeking Spirituality

A Field Guide to Practice

Meredith Gould

D0062521

LITURGICAL PRESS

Collegeville, Minnesota

www.litpress.org

1   2   3   4   5   6   7   8   9

Library of Congress Cataloging-in-Publication Data

Names: Gould, Meredith, 1951– author.
Title: Desperately seeking spirituality : a field guide to practice / Meredith Gould.
Description: Collegeville, Minnesota : Liturgical Press, 2016. | Includes bibliographical references and index.
Identifiers: LCCN 2015046049 (print) | LCCN 2015049891 (ebook) | ISBN 9780814648506 (pbk.) | ISBN 9780814648759 (ebook)
Subjects: LCSH: Spiritual life—Catholic Church.
Classification: LCC BX2350.3 .G68 2016 (print) | LCC BX2350.3 (ebook) | DDC 248.4—dc23
LC record available at http://lccn.loc.gov/2015046049

"Gould's wit and simplicity of style opens this text up to all who are in desperate need of some spirituality or who need a refresh on what it means to seek after God in our everyday life."

—Rev. Evan M. Dolive
  Author of *Seeking Imperfection: Body Image, Marketing and God*

"You need this book. I need this book. Clergy and laity alike. Believers and seekers both. Those who are prone to orthopraxytosis and those whose meditations are distracted by the cat's horking. You are not alone. With great warmth and wit, Meredith Gould offers a depth of research, a breadth of how-to's and a serious dose of candor to make *Desperately Seeking Spirituality* an invaluable companion for this journey of 'sacred spelunking.' Clean up whatever the cat did, and then it's *inward ho!*"

—Rev. Rachel G. Hackenberg, author of *Sacred Pause* and *Writing to God*

"I am one of the clergy Meredith mentions who is in desperate need of this book and I didn't know that until I read it! *Desperately Seeking Spirituality* provides generous, practical ways to delight in the wonder of this life and God's merciful presence. Especially for those of us for whom spirituality is our profession, this book is a fresh perspective."

—The Rev. Jes Kast-Keat
  Associate Minister, West End Collegiate Church, NYC

"For seekers of every spiritual tradition who hunger to go deeper into the sacred, this book will inspire and invigorate that holy quest."

—The Right Reverend Chilton Knudsen, Retired Episcopal Bishop of Maine

"This is a terrific little book. Meredith Gould has walked the walk and has earned the right to talk about the spiritual path. Here she illumines the wise old Latin adage *Agere Sequitur Esse*, or Doing Follows Being, and inspires us to focus on five essential practices of being: willingness, curiosity, empathy, generosity, and delight. From these inner wells spring all else: spiritual practice, good deeds, peace, gratitude, mercy, and love."

—Michael Leach, author of *Why Stay Catholic? Unexpected Answers to a Life Changing Question*

"As a seeker, I often trudge through drab, austere books, maintaining a respectful distance from the author's voice, in order to glean a kernel of wisdom for my mundane life. I have come to expect pious detachment from truly spiritual people. Meredith Gould shatters those expectations in *Desperately Seeking Spirituality*. Through her essential words, Gould walks beside us, pointing out the delight and suffering in our journey, and cramming each page with vibrant wisdom and insightful humor."

—Rev. Carol Howard Merritt, *Christian Century* columnist and author of *Healing Spiritual Wounds* and *Reframing Hope*

"What sets this book apart from others is its grounding in social science while simultaneously offering accessible, authentic methods to develop a personal spiritual roadmap. Instead of instructing the reader to follow a predetermined route, this guide offers places to pause to consider, reflect and engage in the spiritual landscape."

—Pamela Ressler, MS, RN, HNB-BC
    Founder, StressResources.com
    Faculty, Pain Research, Education and Policy Tufts University School
        of Medicine

"Are your spiritual practices no longer working for you? With her usual witty, clever and concise prose, Meredith Gould charts for readers a refreshing new way to examine the passages through 'dark nights.' She provides suggestions that just may lead you to a deepened sense of being and open your eyes to the sacredness in everyday life."

—Richard Rohr, OFM

"The image of a seeker standing before shelves of books looking bewildered can now be replaced with an image of a seeker happily holding a copy of this book. Meredith Gould has written what will certainly be the go-to volume for many; both those who search for a spiritual practice, and those with a practice, but who wish to go wider and deeper. With her trademark brand of experience-based wisdom infused with humor, the author offers readers smart, practical, and refreshing options as they make their spiritual way."

—Fran Rossi Szpylczyn, blogger, *Give Us This Day* contributing writer

"Meredith Gould has written with candor and insight about what many spiritual seekers have discovered—finding rest in God is not something that can be guaranteed by dedication to the practice of spiritual disciplines. For those of us who've been there, done that, that, and that, and found our souls wearied by the process, *Desperately Seeking Spirituality* offers grace, freedom and practical refreshment."

—Michelle Van Loon, author of *Days Of Yes: How Our Holy Celebrations
    Shape Our Faith* (NavPress, 2016)

For You . . . and also for you.

The feeling remains that God is on the journey, too.

—Saint Teresa of Ávila

Contents

Foreword

Thy sea, O God, is so great, My boat so small.

—Winfred Ernest Garrison,
church historian (1874–1969)

These opening lines from the "Breton Fisherman's Prayer" capture the sense of smallness we feel when faced with both the immensity of the universe and the many concrete situations we confront during our brief existence. Greater awareness of our place within the vast scheme of things can lead us to a sense of wonder or awe . . . when it doesn't scare the bejeebers out of us. And it's a really good place to begin our spiritual journey.

There's lots of debate about spirituality, so I'll explain what it is, at least in my mind. For me, spirituality involves being keenly aware that there's *more*: always more than I can know, more than can be spoken or even dreamed, more than I can perceive and every attempt to do any of these things will fail at some point. Attempts fail because there is, after all, always more and greater than self. But the good news is that I can point to it and tell you how it felt. I can recognize when that awareness is very present, and also when it feels very absent.

Years ago, while visiting a farm in the hinterlands of West Virginia, some friends and I decided to watch the Perseid meteor shower from a hillside pasture. We were able to see the entire Milky Way because there was no perceptible light pollution. It was spectacular. Meteors were abundant that night. Also amazing. A solar flare initiated the appearance of the aurora borealis and although I'd seen it several times, I'd never experienced that level of activity or vibrancy before, nor have I since. That night as I gazed up into the night sky, I felt a profound sense of awe. I sensed the more and greater than self.

Since then I've recognized spiritual experiences in lots of places: in hospital rooms while sitting with the dying; when immersed in creative experiences of great beauty; during the deep silence of contemplative prayer; in the profound quiet of the high desert of New Mexico; watching a whale leap out of the ocean; observing the love of my grandfather for my grandmother during their last years; and especially in the growing awareness (and relief) that I really don't know nearly as much as I once thought I did.

Spirituality can also be appreciated as the journey itself, regardless of destination. The challenges are many, including but not limited to how we cultivate and sustain spiritual awareness with "practices."

In this book, Meredith Gould provides a wonderful variety of insights, observations, and spiritual practices to support seekers. Her experiential knowledge of the spiritual journey with its awesome vistas and treacherous squalls is both enduring and diverse. I can assert this because we met nearly twenty years ago during an iconography workshop I led at a lovely retreat center in Rhode Island. We had a challenging student in that group and Meredith recently reminded me that we connected by way of a bit of mutual eye-rolling. Guilty! I liked her immediately and not only because of that.

During breaks, we discovered many shared experiences and interests, each of them curiously related to our respective spiritual journeys, which, in some ways, couldn't be more different. I'd been engaged in "religious" pursuits since my Irish-Catholic youth. These included being a member of an ecumenical monastic community and then a priest, in addition to being an iconographer. Meredith's spiritual journey, anchored in her Jewish upbringing, has included being part of a yogic community and ministry across Christian denominations. We are fellow travelers in twelve-step recovery and both view service as an essential spiritual practice.

Over the years we've painted together on several occasions and shared a few creative adventures that have included writing and editing books. We both enjoy the rich diversity of life in that vast sea of all things spiritual. And, we both started questioning how spiritual life is lived and expressed.

I, for example, am a whole lot less "religious" or "pious" than I was during my youth and young adulthood. Decades ago, it was all about institutions, buildings, special garments, apparitions and quirky "miracles," titles of honor, prayer books, and rubrics. Now my spiritual life and the practices that support it look quite a bit different and involve ongoing questions like: How might seekers create a sacred space within, making room for mystery and awe, for something "more" and "greater" while navigating deep waters? Which practices will foster an ever-deepening awareness of what often lies hidden in plain sight? How will we know when we get there? *Is* there a *there*?

Perhaps the best way to answer any of these questions is to simply begin with (or return to) what Meredith identifies as the practices of being—willingness, curiosity, empathy, generosity, and delight. Without a doubt it includes cultivating more awareness about self-care on the journey!

When it comes to these things, Meredith knows her stuff and, in this book for seekers, blesses others with the stuff she knows. She gets it and I believe this guide will support you in getting it as well. So, turn the page and read on. I wish you traveling mercies.

Fr. Peter Pearson
Iconographer
Scranton, PA
http://www.peterpearsonicons.com

Preface

Depending on who you ask I was either "always" or "never" like this and by "like this," I mean spiritual. There were some hints along the way during childhood and early adulthood, but my impetus to seek something greater than and beyond self kicked into gear during my late thirties. And only then because of a near-complete meltdown of body and mind . . . while working at an ad agency.

There is no shortage of stories from that period and the following decades of spiritual spelunking. I haven't written much about those adventures, mostly because I prefer face-to-face conversations about them. If we ever meet, please feel free to ask about when liquid light flowed through my hands (especially in the presence of truth), unexpected glossolalia spilled out of my mouth (usually in the bathtub), music of the spheres became audible (when I was quiet), and verses from Scripture appeared (in dreams).

Go ahead and ask me about why my belief in the resurrection became unshakeable after meeting a Filipino psychic surgeon, about close encounters of the yoga ashram and guru kind, about the visit from Jesus that shook me up and the angel encounter that calmed me down.

Fearfully and wonderfully weird, all of it. And apparently necessary to get my full attention, although I did kindasorta ask for it by praying, "prove it" without ceasing.

The mysterious mystical tour continued after I was baptized at age forty-three and even after logging a solid chunk of time in twelve-step recovery. My acute awareness of the sacred began dissipating during my fifties. By then, I'd become involved with church and traditional spiritual practices.

I loved the comfort of the liturgical structure for worship as well as the calendar year. Traditional practices provided a tidy container for spiritual inquiry. I prayed Vespers and Compline, practiced *lectio divina*. Never got into praying the rosary but did bead lots of them as a form of contemplative prayer. I took myself on regular walks on a blessedly local labyrinth. I went on icon painting retreats and rediscovered Christianity's version of *tratak sadhana*. Not content with simply echoing the cadence of Gregorian chant, I learned how to read shape notes.

In the world of church-the-building I joined the choir, served as a cantor until it felt like performance rather than prayer; served as a lector and eucharistic minister. Loved all of it. Welcomed the growing pains. Recognized the predictable plateau. Got lulled into a stupor punctuated by short bursts of distress as I realized that instead of keeping me awake, traditional practices were putting me to sleep. I could barely detect the sacred in everyday life, let alone in the context of church-the-building. Oh the dismay, followed by the grief of comprehending the extent to which ancient practices had gutted my spiritual life.

I couldn't be the only longtime seeker in this increasingly unfit spiritual condition, so, desperately seeking a reality check, I used social media to post this query: *"Which of the traditional/venerable spiritual practices do you think you *should* practice but can't because they 'don't work' for you?"* Oh the dismay, followed by relief of seeing that the swiftly provided list included regular Morning Prayer, *lectio divina*, centering prayer, labyrinth walking, fasting, and meditation. Who had the most to say in the least positive terms about these practices?

Clergy. But not in public—those comments I received via the back channel and for weeks after I'd posted the question.

I became reenergized. Discovering why and when traditional practices stopped working for those most inclined to use them would become my focus. And because writing has always been a gateway to spiritual growth, I decided to write a book—the one you're reading right now.

Desperately Seeking Spirituality is about embracing a broader definition of practice that shifts focus from doing to being. Here's a brief guide to this guide:

- *Section I: In the Beginning* provides a framework for understanding why spiritual development is described as a lifelong journey. Chapters in this section draw on sociology, behavioral psychology, learning theory, and the history of religion to reveal why and when traditional spiritual practices might stop working . . . for lots of people. These chapters also offer explanations about why and when "practices of being" will more effectively fuel the spiritual journey.

- *Section II: The Spiritual Practices of Being* focuses on what I identify as five essential practices of being: willingness, curiosity, empathy, generosity, and delight. Chapters in this section explain why these are spiritual practices, identify psychospiritual barriers to practicing them, and provide four suggestions for hands-and-heart-on practice. I've used a tips format for "Practicing the Practice" so you won't have to wade through pages of prose to find suggestions for getting started.

- *Section III: Self-Care on the Journey* is where you'll find chapters about recognizing and mitigating inevitable conditions like spiritual awakening flameout and spiritual practice burnout. Included here are chapters about embracing solitude as well as developing a more nuanced understanding of relaxation and rest.

Each chapter includes questions to help you explore attitudes, beliefs, and behaviors that might be running you spiritually ragged. I urge you to physically write out your responses because there's a boatload of reliable research to explain why the physical act of writing helps deliver content to the brain. In addition, please consider dedicating a special journal to documenting your experiences with the practices of being.

Please read the endnotes. Although this is clearly not an academic book, I include lots of citations and resources (with online links) in the endnotes. Plus I always use endnotes for commentary that I haven't jammed into the main text, some percentage of which is the snarktastic stuff I mutter to myself as well as a few not-so-hidden "Easter eggs."

My prayerful hope is that what I've rediscovered comes as relief. I invite you to explore the practices of being, even before you can no longer stomach traditional ones and after you (maybe) return to them. Hackneyed but true: spiritual life is a journey. I hope this map works as well for you as it has for me. Inward ho! Again.

Acknowledgments

Writing is a spiritual discipline that requires solitude but also benefits from being practiced in community. Keenly aware of being the beneficiary of both, I am grateful beyond measure to this spiritually wise and editorially savvy community of first readers: Rev. Aric Clark, Katy Dunigan, Ruth Harrigan, and Regina Heater. Ruth has guided me through self-inflicted authorial angst for nearly a decade; can't imagine publishing anything without her love and support.

Special thanks to coach extraordinaire Rev. Laurie J. Ferguson, PhD, and acupuncturist Allyson Jones, LCSW, LAc, both of whom provided remarkably congruent observations about my creative process and counsel about embracing it, albeit from different perspectives. Allyson's was more pointed. Yes, I did just do that.

Extra special thanks to Rev. Canon Dan Webster (a.k.a., my husband) for generosity of spirit and his powerful power of example in the domain of disciplined spiritual practice. Dan also knows when to provide the gifts of silence, solitude, and sushi.

Thanks to social media, I received ongoing public encouragement from many people within multiple online communities, sacred and secular. I received reminders about self-care and soul-nourishing snark via the "back channel" from:

Rev. Jason Chesnut, John Deuel, Neal F. Fischer, Rev. David Hansen, Rev. Sue Lang, Rev. Carol Howard Merritt, Jen Sandmann, Mike Sevilla, MD, Fran Rossi Szpylczyn, and Colleen Young. I'll let you figure out who among them are my dearly beloved snarkmeisters. This was yet another book whose writing process benefitted from sanity-restoring laughs provided by @UnvirtuousAbbey and @JesusofNaz316.

I remain blessed by the editorial team at Liturgical Press for their real presence from book proposal through production: Andy Edwards, Barry Hudock, Stephanie Lancour, and Michelle Verkuilen. Speaking of production, thanks abiding to a rocking-amazing team that includes: Colleen Stiller, Stephanie Nix, and Julie Surma. Extra kudos to cover designer Stefan Killen for the fabulous result of a delightful process.

Always and forever, thanks be to God.

SECTION I

In the Beginning

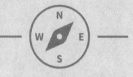

Chapter 1

About That Spiritual Journey

As a Seeker, you already have lots of experience-based knowledge about the search for meaning and connection beyond self. You also already know that spiritual growth is not a whole lot of fun. Really, who posts "starting my spiritual journey" to their calendar (or Facebook profile) with a slappy-happy emoticon or emoji?[1] More often than not, a bold declaration of "Inward ho!" is soon followed by whimpering, "Inward whoa."

To make matters more . . . interesting . . . spiritual awakening, which happens in stages, is also cyclical. Forward movement involves going backward, as in revisiting all sorts of things. "Look back, but don't stare" is common counsel among those in the spiritual program of twelve-step recovery. Plus, there's no proof that we're done when we're dead, which is why even if you already know lots about spiritual development, it might be comforting to review what's involved.

You can find maps of the spiritual journey that identify a dozen stops and detours, but the trajectory is always the same and involves moving from false assumptions to embracing what is; from shattered self to integrated identity; from self-absorption to serving others. If you're reading this book, you've probably already cycled through all identifiable and predictable phases of the spiritual journey at least once. Still, for your consideration, here's my four-stage description of the journey.

Stage I: Wake-Up Call

Waking up is hard to do, so something needs to trigger an alarm. In the presence of anything less drastic, humans will hit the cosmic snooze button and go back to sleep. Spiritual awakening begins when something happens to challenge life as lived up until that point.

Typically this "something" is catastrophic, such as a dire medical diagnosis or near-death experience (NDE), relationship and career devastation, mental or emotional breakdown, financial ruin. Fundamental beliefs about what is right, true, and tolerable are trashed.

Big messes beg big questions: Why is this crap happening to me? Now what? Why am I even here? When will I be done with Earth duty?

Everything feels very personal and horribly private. Maybe it's time to check out that God thing or, if the word "God" is a barrier, a higher power or something not created, orchestrated, and conducted by you.

Stage II: Into the Darkness

Has that wake-up call really been answered? Is surrender to divine providence immediate and complete? Certainly not before engaging in rigorous self-examination, the work of forgiveness, and accepting whatever cannot be changed.

During this stage, rough places don't become level for what seems like an eternity. And not the in-the-loving-embrace-of-God kind of eternity, but the is-this-thing-over-yet type.

What we think is our path to God, may not be our path to God. Turns out the "dark night of the soul" lasts much longer than one night and the metaphor is as accurate as it is lyrical. Feelings of wanting to withdraw and isolate while questioning everything are typical at this stage. Holy hissy fits of biblical proportion become a regular occurrence and you want to smack the next person who suggests that God can handle your anger because your anger is so epic. Change is no longer an option. Spiritual transformation becomes a burning desire— emphasis on burning.[2]

Is It Spiritual Change . . .

- You review the past and are willing to make midcourse adjustments that may include religious affiliation.
- You tinker with some of what doesn't enhance spiritual growth.
- Your attitudes, beliefs, behaviors, and habits shift, but you're basically an improved version of yourself—and you know you can opt out of change.

. . . Or Is It Spiritual Transformation?

- You have a seemingly sudden desire to jettison whatever doesn't enhance spiritual growth, which may include religious affiliation.
- You completely ditch what doesn't enhance spiritual growth and radically reorganize your life.
- You move forward with new identity and sense of purpose. You couldn't go back to who you were, even if you wanted to—which you don't.

Stage III: Connecting the Dots

Eventually, anxiety is reframed as excitement and confusion turns to enhanced clarity about everything. Life has newly discovered meaning and purpose. Joy and contentment emerge and endure for longer than a few hours or days. The unreal becomes very real, darkness becomes light, and eternal life becomes more than lovely promise.[3] You know, feel, and see how God really is in all things and everywhere.

Existing relationships either become healthier or recognized as dysfunctional and ditched. If previously split or severed, the body-mind-spirit connection is restored; integrity (i.e., wholeness) becomes a felt experience. Environmental consciousness starts emerging as a result of realizing how all beings share a sacred heritage, if not necessarily the same religious expression thereof.

Studying, taking classes, attending workshops, going on pilgrimages and retreats is typical at this stage. Also typical at this stage: exploring a variety of spiritual practices, searching for the tried-and-true form of prayer or meditation that will bring you into closer contact with the Almighty.

Age, Aging, and Spiritual Growth

When it comes to spiritual growth, how significant is chronological age? Turns out, not very. A spiritual awakening triggered by a life-threatening illness, near-death and other non-ordinary consciousness experiences, or radical challenges to so-called normal life can happen at any age.

Somewhat more significant is gender coupled with traditional life cycle changes. For example, ciswomen[4] beyond childbearing age and finished with daily child-rearing activities seem to be more free to focus on spiritual growth.[5]

Meanwhile, aging itself is being viewed as a spiritual process partly but not entirely because of proximity to end of life. Swedish sociologist Lars Tornstam has developed an elegant theory of gerotranscendence to highlight existential and spiritual aspects of aging. Check it out, especially if you're approaching the sixth decade of life or have friends already there.[6]

Stage IV: Reaching Out and Beyond Self

Despite having settled into a regular spiritual practice and being on superb speaking terms with God, a certain restlessness emerges. This disturbance in the body-mind-spirit field feels different from the soulish hunger that initially promoted the spiritual journey. Big questions get bigger: Why am I here? What am I called to do? Other people—their needs and sorrows—are becoming more intriguing. You're realizing that "it" isn't even about you. Spiritual life, it turns out, is ultimately about understanding and acting upon the knowledge that all beings share a sacred heritage.

Empathy flourishes as a result of understanding sacred interconnectivity and you're able to be compassionate. The shift from fear to love is more durable at this stage, as is acting for the greater good (not to mention understanding that there *is* a greater good). Across all religious traditions, the ability to love and the desire to serve others is considered evidence of spiritual maturity, and so is understanding the value of community for doing and being.

But don't get too comfy. Annoying reminder: spiritual awakening is a process, not a one-time enlightenment event. It's not unusual to arrive at what looks like the triumphant end to an arduous journey, only to end up back at what seems like the beginning.

As anyone on this lifelong journey will tell you and you probably already know, it's all fun and revelation, until it's not. The spiritual journey is frequently difficult—often discouraging, occasionally frightening, ongoing.

Good news: hunkering down for another round (or few more) gets easier. Wake-up calls become more like tinkling bells than clanging gongs; dark nights give way to dark naps of the soul. Better to view these as opportunities to grow in wisdom, understanding, and spiritual maturity rather than a cosmic pain in the butt.

KNOW THYSELF—ABOUT THAT SPIRITUAL JOURNEY

While you don't have to worry about getting lost when faith is your compass, it's good to periodically review your progress on the spiritual journey. It's cyclical and never-ending but nevertheless, you are . . . where? Check it out by asking:

- At what stage of the spiritual journey am I right now? Where was I last year?

- Which life challenges and losses have generated my greatest spiritual growth?

- How has my spiritual journey changed as I've logged more time on the planet?

How Firm Is Your Foundation?

According to twentieth-century psychologist Abraham Maslow, motivation is based on a hierarchy of needs. Growth, Maslow argued, cannot happen before survival is reasonably assured. The epitome of growth, which he termed "self-actualization," includes commonly recognized features of spiritual awareness.

Maslow's hierarchy of needs is a developmental model worth revisiting to consider how the experience of having some needs met, but not others, might affect the trajectory of your spiritual journey.

Maslow's Hierarchy of Needs

Level I: Physiological Needs

    air, water, food, clothing, shelter, sleep, sex

Level II: Safety and Security Needs

    order, stability, certainty, routine, familiarity, protection from fear and disease, physical safety, economic security, freedom from threat

Level III: Social Needs

    love, acceptance, belonging, affection

Level IV: Esteem Needs

    respect and recognition from others, self-respect, a sense of prestige

Level V: Self-Actualization Needs

    "peak" experiences, fulfilling a sense of self and calling, opportunities for learning and creating at higher levels

Chapter 2

About Those Spiritual Practices

Once upon a time, a knowledgeable, trusted, well-meaning someone told you to pick and stick with a spiritual practice. Perhaps, during a period of feeling like crap without ceasing you read something in a lifestyle magazine about exploring "ancient practices" to get an interior life.[1]

After that, you read a few books, ones with checklists and exercises not unlike, but not exactly like, this one. You studied systems for classifying time-honored ways of finding the divine.[2]

Coming to Terms with Terms

For centuries, people of faith assumed that disciplined religiosity would automatically deepen spiritual life. Spiritual practices were, by definition, religious ones that happened within the context of church—the social institution, if not always the actual building.

By the twenty-first century, disconnects between church affiliation and spiritual behavior had become impossible to ignore.[3] Using the term "religious" to characterize spiritual

---

practices no longer made a whole lot of sense to a whole lot
of people. Am I the only one who knows clergy and church
leaders who make haste to assert that they're more spiritual
than religious? I think not.

These days, even people who actively participate in church-
based worship and embrace religious doctrine use the term
"spiritual practices" to describe intentional actions that generate and support a spiritual experience *a.k.a.* a connection to the
divine or, in the reliably useful words of twelve-step recovery,
an "awareness of a Power greater than ourselves."[4]

Thus inspired, you probably enrolled in a class or attended a
weekend workshop, ultimately plunging into weeklong retreats
for advanced practitioners. You may have gotten certified to
teach other people how to practice. You listened to tapes when
tapes were a thing, then podcasts once those became popular.

Depending on the state of online technology when you got
started and your comfort with it, you likely participated in
virtual online communities for prayer and lively conversations
about spiritual life.[5] Eventually, you were meditating, centering praying, Gregorian chanting, *lectio divina*-ing, labyrinth
walking, and gazing at icons that you, yes you, painted.[6]

The traditional practices that helped fuel your journey
have a venerable track record; there are valid compelling reasons why they've stood the test of time. The rituals and rules
structuring them create a predictable and therefore safe container for sacred spelunking (see Chapter 4: Sorting Through
Structure).

The repetitive nature of some practices, like chanting or
praying with beads, serves to calm internal chaos, as do ones
anchored in silence, like meditation and contemplation. Over
the centuries, entire communities have emerged to teach and
support the sustained practice of practice.

And there are equally compelling reasons why, especially over an extended period of time, traditional spiritual practices might start feeling like an irritating waste of time—and not because you're doing them wrong.

True, we humans do have a pesky tendency toward self-sabotage, especially when it comes to sticking with things that involve following rules and accountability to any kind of authority. But it's equally likely that a once-loved practice has stopped working for you because it has become horridly out of sync with the shape-shifting realities of your life.

For example, you could be at a different point in your career, one that requires more focus and energy in the external world. Family responsibilities have intensified because your children and/or aging parents deserve more time and energy. Changes in your physical health might be having an impact on your ability to continue particular practices, especially ones involving sitting or walking or gazing at anything for more than a few minutes. (As someone living with fibromyalgia for three decades, I can attest to the grim reality of having to rethink practices involving too much, not enough, or, at times, any physical motion no matter how subtle.)

Perhaps the practice you chose or that was recommended for you no longer correlates at all with your personality type or dominant learning style. If you're an extrovert, you're inspired and energized by people (preferably in big boisterous groups), so sitting in silent meditation is devitalizing. If you're a visual-kinesthetic learner, you're frustrated to the point of silent screaming by practices involving oral recitation from memory. If you're an aural[7] learner, *lectio divina* or any practice that requires reading a text seems at best onerous, at worst punitive.

Learning Styles and Spiritual Practices

Identifying the primary ways you learn will help you do just about everything with significantly less anxiety and frustration, including spiritual practices. Here's a super-short guide to learning styles:[8]

- People who are always on the move, enjoy physical activities, and prefer hands-on instruction are primarily *kinesthetic*.
- People who love talking, singing, listening, and prefer verbal instruction are primarily *auditory*.
- People who think in images, are sensitive to nuances of color, texture, and shape, and would rather read instructions are primarily *visual*.

No one is purely visual, auditory, or kinesthetic, but a blend of each with one being dominant. What does this have to do with spiritual practices?

It's entirely possible (read: probable) that the spiritual practices you don't like and can't sustain might be at odds with your learning style. Your inability to do, never mind experience any spiritual benefits from, traditional practices might also be explained by learning disabilities (e.g., dyslexia, auditory/visual processing disorders).

Forcing yourself to practice something that's out of whack with your learning style or neurological makeup is *not* a sign of your amazingly awesome spiritual devotion. Consider that it might, in fact, be evidence of incipient masochism.

Learning Styles and Traditional Spiritual Practices			
	Visual seeing/ reading	*Auditory* listening/ speaking	*Kinesthetic* touching/ doing/moving
Adoration/Contemplation	√		
Chanting/Singing		√	√
Daily Office/Prayer	√	√	
Icon Gazing/Iconography	√		√
Labyrinth Walking			√
Lectio Divina/Study	√	√	
Meditation/Centering Prayer		√	

Another possibility is you got so gung ho that you've practiced your way into burnout (see Chapter 10: Spiritual Practice Burnout).

Devoting time to discover more about your disconnects with traditional practices will be time well spent—a spiritual practice in and of itself. Going back in time, try to recall:

- *Why you began any of these traditional practices:* What felt missing from your life? What were you seeking? What needed to stop? What needed to happen? Who were you? Who did you hope to become?

- *When you began any of these traditional practices:* How old were you? Where did you live? Were you economically self-sufficient? What sort of work occupied your time? Did you have a family and friendship network?

Throughout the ages and across all spiritual traditions—Western and Eastern—the promised results of spiritual practice are remarkably similar, as are many of the practices themselves.[9] The short list of promised results: love, joy, peace, patience, kindness, generosity, faithfulness, gentleness, and self-control (Gal 5:22-23).

For a change try focusing on actually *being* rather than *doing* stuff that promises to get you there eventually. Rather than praying for generosity of spirit, practice being generous. Rather than meditating on compassion, practice being empathetic.

And unless you believe the intellectual exercise will be at all productive and fun, do not squander precious energy wondering which comes first, the being or the doing. Instead, scrutinize your personal point of entry to spiritual growth. If all your "doing" hasn't enhanced "being," consider switching vectors to become the spiritual self you wish to be in this world.[10]

Give yourself permission to acknowledge which sacred practices have become restrictive and restricting—when they've closed off rather than opened up pathways to God.

KNOW THYSELF—
ASSESSING SPIRITUAL PRACTICES

Ready to abandon any or all of those traditional spiritual practices? Maybe you are, but first take a closer look at your reasons for ditching them. After making a list of all the practices you've given a go, answer these questions for each one:

- For how long and how regularly did I practice?

- Why did I stop this practice or why do I want to stop it now?

- What might have inspired or helped me continue this practice?

Chapter 3

Powerful Paradox

Just when you think you're making real progress and could possibly be considered somewhat almost spiritually mature, you start getting super-confused by the paradoxical quality of core teachings. So what if these paradoxes have been there all along? Now they loom larger in your conscious awareness and seem to be getting in your way.

What you once welcomed as pleasantly perplexing truisms have morphed into profoundly annoying mind-twisters. You're ready to fuel a fire pit with every aphorism-loaded poster, T-shirt, and coffee mug you've ever treasured.

Stuff you've been reading for years—sacred texts, wisdom teachings, daily devotionals—seem more irritating than inspiring. Not at all comforting. Quite the opposite. Where, pray tell, is the comfort in struggling to reconcile contradictory statements that are supposed to reveal deep, complex, eternal truths?

You can start by finding comfort in knowing that by definition a paradox makes no intuitive sense, cannot be swiftly or easily understood, and generates profound confusion, even among longtime spiritual seekers.[1]

You might also be comforted by knowing that wrestling with paradox is an inescapable aspect of spiritual growth. Every religious tradition has core teachings firmly fixed in paradox. In at least one Eastern tradition, pondering paradox is itself considered a key practice.[2]

Christian living is packed with paradox, most of which was introduced by Jesus, who almost never passed up an opportunity to dumbfound dimwitted disciples with counterintuitive teachings, often embedded in equally confusing parables. (I, for one, cannot read the Gospel According to Matthew without imagining crowds muttering, "Can't we just get our loaves and fishes and get out of here?")

This didactic tradition continues on in the letters of St. Paul, through writings of church fathers and mothers, in wisdom attributed to the saints and delivered these days by spiritual teachers, popular poets, and bumper sticker copywriters.

You probably already know which paradoxes make faith the assurance of things hoped for but not necessarily seen. Here they are again, in no logical order:

- Don't worry about anything and trust in God's grace and mercy. Go right ahead and ask your God in heaven for what you want.

- Give to receive. Gain everything by surrendering all.

- The least and last will become the first and greatest.

- Becoming lost is one way to be found.

- Pay attention to the small still voice within. Follow the great commandments.

- History is instructive. God makes all things new.

- God is unknowable, beyond our understanding. God is everywhere and very near.

- Seeking and finding God is a journey that could take forty days, forty years, or a full corporeal lifetime. Stay steady and focused with your eye on the prize. Trust in the slow work of God.[3] You can be changed in a moment.

Seeking the Divine is in and of itself paradoxical—a waltz with wonder and a pounding headache. You're in excellent good company if you think (or mutter): "These paradoxes make no sense and therefore cannot be right, and if they cannot be right, how can they possibly be true?" But by definition, paradox is exactly all that: counterintuitive, right, and true. What else might be right, true, and devoid of logic? Mystery, that comfy refuge of all Seekers.[4]

Surrender Is Not Giving Up

If you get squirrelly when you read or hear the word "surrender," it's probably because you think it means giving up, caving in, or otherwise capitulating without dignity or choice. Often it does, but not when used in the context of spiritual life.

In spiritual writings, the word *surrender* refers to embracing circumstances just as they are, releasing a white-knuckled grip on wishful thinking. (Extra spiritual points granted for noting how circumstances are always in flux.)

Even the most conscientious spiritual seekers have been known to confuse surrender with giving up, especially when big ego stakes are involved. Letting go is involved no matter which word you use, but at least "surrender" is a word with spiritual gravitas.

Oh those powerful pesky paradoxes.

Try not to worry too much about figuring out the core paradoxes of spiritual life, at least not durably so because, really, you cannot. Leave that frustrating fun to theologians and philosophers. Instead, be grateful for fleeting glimmers of understanding that you should feel free to reframe as moments of transcendence. (Pile up enough of these and you, too, may write a spiritual memoir.)

Paradoxically, the only way out is through the thicket of thinking. Begin by reframing paradox as complementary rather than contradictory. Move beyond observing to experiencing, and then to welcoming the dynamic tension of opposites as gateways to spiritual growth. Know that when it comes to spiritual life, going in circles is one way to move forward.

Reframing as Another Gateway to Consciousness

Reframing is an effective cognitive technique for reviewing and revising less-than-helpful or downright toxic ways of conceptualizing so-called reality. It involves actively shifting the frame of reference from negative to positive. As a result, meaning shifts from negative to positive, along with the attitudes, beliefs, and emotions that go along with it. One of the most familiar and well-worn reframes is this one: "It's not a problem, it's an opportunity."

If you think reframing is just a clever gloss or mind game, think again.[5] Because it involves a purposeful shift in consciousness, reframing could itself be reframed as a gateway to spiritual growth, a spiritual practice, and probably your best conceptual tactic for dealing with boredom and routine. Notice what happens when you reframe the former as "serenity" and the latter as "comfort."

I recommend viewing paradox as fodder for practicing willingness, curiosity, and possibly the delight that comes with not knowing anything in typical ways of knowing. And then, choosing practices that will allow you to embrace paradox without stopping the journey. As if you could, after getting this far.

The Incredible Weirdness of Time

As if the core spiritual paradoxes don't mess with our perceptions enough, time and timing are already messed up beyond predictable recognition, thanks, in part, to twenty-first-century technology.

Online digital technology has made everything faster. As a result, we want near-instant response to every email, text, tweet, and post we send forth. A twinkling of an eye seems too slow. Speed and real or near-real time response challenges our conventional understanding of time that can be measured (a.k.a., *chronos*).

Teachings about how time cannot be measured (a.k.a., *kairos*) have become yet another challenge for twenty-first-century Seekers. Once again, the way out is through. In this instance I recommend practicing curiosity instead of getting caught up in confusion, keeping in mind that God's time and timing supersedes all.

KNOW THYSELF—EMBRACING PARADOX

At first, wrestling with paradox seemed like a great idea, but what started out as a driver-motivator to spiritual growth became a barrier-deterrent. You could not reconcile the contradictions, nor could you reconcile their irreconcilable nature. Let's try to make spiritual paradoxes thrum gently in the background by consciously (and paradoxically) focusing on them, asking:

- How, if at all, has my tolerance for spiritual paradox changed over time?

- Which of the core spiritual paradoxes generates the most anxiety for me and why?

- Which of the core spiritual paradoxes might be worth exploring in more depth? (Note: Do *not* choose the one that triggers an anxiety attack.)

Chapter 4

Sorting Through Structure

Can't stomach structure? Gee that's too bad, because it's always going to be there. Always. And I'm confident in asserting this because I'm a (social) scientist. Ghostbusters . . . anyone?[1]

Here's a reality check from anthropology and sociology: all groups across cultures create structure at the macro level of society, the micro level of conversation, and every level of connection in between. Even the most seemingly chaotic group will eventually establish an organized network of positions, roles, and rules to survive. Structure provides and reinforces meaning, ensures coherence, and makes continuity possible.

Over time, networks become formalized as social institutions.[2] We find these core, or what sociologists label as "primary," social institutions in all known societies: family, government, economy, education, and religion. While form may vary within each primary social institution, function does not.

Religion is a terrific example—and not just because this book is about spiritual growth. Religion, the social institution that defines and regulates how humans deal with the supernatural (among other things), takes many forms as well as multiple expressions of each form (a.k.a., denomination)

23

within any one religion.[3] Christianity is especially flush with denominations often in conflict, something that I, coming to Christianity as an adult,[4] experience as disturbing, given that You Are All One in Christ Jesus thing (Gal 3:28).[5] Moving right along . . .

Additional social structures emerge and become formalized over time. Simple customs (mores) and informal yet agreed upon ways of behaving (norms) eventually become an established system of rules (laws).

Turning again to the example of religion, some customs and traditions (e.g., sacramentals) have given rise to the formal directives (a.k.a., rubrics) for structuring ritual (e.g., liturgy).[6] What was once a simple gathering for conversation and a shared meal became, over time, embedded within a formal ritual (Mass or Holy Communion) with rules about who may bless, break, and distribute bread. And that's just one rather splendid example.

Structure to enforce structure? Yes indeed. And when it comes to religion, there's yet another layer of structure that might start out as merely bothersome and end up becoming almost intolerable: structures for spiritual practice.

Orthopraxytosis[7]

Or-tho-prax-y-to-sis
[awr-th*uh*-prak-see-toe-sis]
noun

A toxic condition characterized by extreme adherence to orthopraxy ("right practice"), generally the result of an unholy convergence of theological study and brain biochemistry. Symptoms include overwrought reactivity in response to violations (real and perceived) of liturgy and spiritual practices.

Every religious tradition has created structures for spiritual practice. Since practices are remarkably similar across religious traditions, structures for practice are too.

No matter how many prayer times are considered "right practice" (a.k.a., orthopraxy), every religious tradition mandates prayer at the endpoints of every day.[8] Formal meditation, whether it opens with a gong, chime, or chant, involves structured focus in silence. Structure, then, is a key feature of spiritual practice. Here are more examples:

- *The Liturgy of the Hours*, a structure for praying throughout the day, includes a schedule of times for prayer as well as one for content that's linked to the liturgical calendar and Lectionary.

- *Lectio divina*, a practice for contemplating Scripture, is structured to: (1) begin with quiet preparation (*silencio*) before (2) reading (*lectio*) and then (3) meditating on Scripture (*meditatio*) preparatory to (4) entering into dialogue with God (*oratio*) and (5) resting in God's presence in and through Scripture (*contemplatio*).

- *The Benedictine Rule*, a structure for practicing Christian life, is organized to balance prayer, work, study, hospitality, and renewal.

- *The Examen*, an Ignatian form of night prayer for recalling God's presence throughout the day, is structured to: (1) begin with expressing gratitude for the day's events as preparatory to (2) reviewing the day and then (3) acknowledging and asking forgiveness for what went wrong, before (4) contemplating what to do differently and more in alignment with God's will in the day ahead.

Let Us Pray? There's an App for That

Online digital technology makes it possible for anyone to pray in alignment with traditional structures (and some that are not) on smartphones, tablets, and other types of computers.

Last time I used Google to search "apps for praying" it took .43 seconds for ~ 2,200,000 results to show up. When I refined the search as "apps for praying in community," ~ 1,420,000 results popped up in .41 seconds. These results included links to apps for creating prayer lists, submitting prayer requests, finding communities devoted exclusively to prayer as well as communities for which prayer is just one among many spiritual practices.

Type "apps for spiritual growth" and "apps for spiritual practices" into the search bar on your browser or into Google Play (Android) or Apple Store/iTunes (iOS) and see what shows up. Consider practicing curiosity when you come across apps that give you the dogmatic creeps.

So. Much. Structure.

Yes, structure is an unavoidable, persistent, and durable feature of spiritual practice, regardless of religion.[9] Still, you don't like—or want—all that structure at this point in your spiritual life.

So now what?

First, remember that you're a Seeker, so whatever you don't like about spiritual life is fair and necessary fodder for inquiry, especially if it has become an impediment to spiritual growth. Sooner or later you'll need to figure out (1) what you don't like, (2) why you don't like it, and (3) what might help you like it better.

Structure Without Ceasing

Spend any time in or around church, especially in a position involving liturgy, and you'll swiftly encounter good people of faith who come across as rigid, unyielding, and annoying gatekeepers of church rubrics.

These are our beloved sisters and brothers in Christ who go ape-crazy if the wrong altar linens are used, candles are lit in the wrong order, someone didn't bow at the right time or place, or some part of liturgy was audible when it should have been *sotto voce* (or the other way around). Is this a manifestation of fidelity or . . . brain biochemistry?

While psychologists and psychiatrists agree that obsessive-compulsive behaviors may emerge because of family system situations, it's also an accepted medical fact that OCD is related to brain biochemistry.[10]

Wait, what? This describes you? If you find yourself moving beyond take-it-or-leave-it preference to what feels like an uncontrollable need for structure, get a consult with a mental health professional specializing in anxiety disorders.

Figure it out sooner. Like now would be a most excellent time to practice curiosity about what's really going on with you (see Chapter 6: Curiosity). Is structure the source of your angst or is it more accurately:

- *Routine:* Are you peeved about structure or routine? You're swiftly and easily bored, and nothing bores you as swiftly and easily as doing anything over and over again without variation. But don't you brush your teeth at least once a day without grousing? What else, regularly done, is no big irritating deal because you view it as a helpful habit? Conversely, what works perfectly well without necessarily being routinized?

- *Rules:* Are you peeved about structure or the prospect of having to follow rules and then being scolded if you don't? Wherever there are rules, there's usually a mechanism for enforcement. You don't have a particularly high (or perhaps any) tolerance for authority, let alone obedience to it. But don't you follow some rules because they make life easier? Do you know the rules well enough to understand (and care about) the consequences of breaking them? And surely you've heard this great axiom of religious life, "It's easier to get forgiveness than permission."

- *Complexity:* Are you peeved about structure or complexity? The structure for practice is so complex that it eclipses substance. You can't remember the sequence of prayers and your breviary ribbons are a tangled mess. These days you sit your butt down throughout worship because kneeling and bowing and breast-beating and making the sign of the cross is just too much. "'Tis a Gift to Be Simple" is your favorite hymn.

And so, what's really bugging you? Is it truly the structure itself, or is it routine, rules, and complexity? If it's any or all of those things, stop squandering precious energy bemoaning structure. Instead, use that energy to futz with the routines, rules, and complexity of traditional practices. Love the Divine Office but don't love mornings? Skip Matins. Love praying the rosary but can't remember which Mysteries go with which days? Contemplate whichever Mystery the Spirit calls you to pray even if it's on the "wrong" day.

Still too much work and energy? Go ahead and take a break from the traditional practices and reorganize daily life to support your practice of being willing, curious, empathetic, generous, and delighted.

KNOW THYSELF—STRUCTURE

Love structure and can't get enough of it? Hate structure and want to ignore it? Not sure whether you love it, hate it, or have settled into blissful indifference? Update your personal reality by answering these questions about rules, ritual, and routine:

- What comes to mind and gut when I encounter structures and rules?

- In which circumstances and under what conditions do I generally find structure helpful?

- Which structures might I need to support spiritual practices that are focused on being?

SECTION II

The Spiritual Practices of Being

Chapter 5

Willingness

Spiritual growth involves changing perceptions, attitudes, and behaviors. It's that annoyingly simple but not at all easy because humans aren't especially keen on change. Even long-time Seekers aspiring to total transformation can be remarkably resistant to changing what they think, do, and even where they want to sit when gathering with other Seekers.

Nearly thirty years ago, some of us justified our arrested psychospiritual development by reciting this affirmation like a sacred mantra: "I am perfect in my imperfection." I did, too, until I realized that my imperfections sucked and I needed to make some radical changes. More than one person bluntly offered this compelling option: "Change or die." Guess which option has seemed much more attractive at times.

So, what's a Seeker to do?

Commit to the practice of willingness. Your conscious practice of willingness will involve ditching denial, rejecting resistance, facing fear, and becoming open to the Great Cosmic Whatever. Intentionally. On purpose. For real. You'll commit to saying "yes" when you don't know and cannot possibly predict the outcome. No willingness, no change.

Here's some good news about the practicalities of practicing willingness: You don't have to *do* or *like* or *accept* or *believe anything* to practice this practice successfully. You just have to be *open* to facing obstacles blocking your spiritual growth, especially any you've created that no longer serve any good purpose on Earth or in heaven. Willingness involves *becoming* amenable to:

- confronting personality quirks that have become barriers to curiosity, empathy, generosity, and delight;

- renouncing skepticism about anything that cannot be seen and known in conventional ways;

- resisting the brainiacal urge to intellectualize . . . everything;

- accepting whatever constitutes current reality and being at peace with what's happening—or not happening;

- releasing long-held and possibly erroneous beliefs about what you're supposed to be doing with "your one wild and precious life";[1]

- feeling a wider and deeper range of emotions as well as their sacred source and meaning;

- understanding that with a more nuanced and deeper awareness of all creation comes sadness, disappointment, grief, and confusion—at first;

- recognizing how body and mind are connected, and the perils of pretending they aren't (see Chapter 10: Spiritual Practice Burnout);

- asking for and receiving guidance, coaching, and perhaps even correction, especially from unexpected and possibly previously unwelcomed sources; and

- questioning if, when, and how institutionalized religion supports or undermines your connection with God.

Fear

Sometimes fear is a barrier to willingness because it's **F**alse **E**vidence **A**ppearing **R**eal. Sometimes fear really does reveal a lack of faith. Sometimes fear is a valuable warning signal that danger lies ahead and it's time to proceed with extreme caution. Or sometimes what feels like fear is actually overwhelming awe in the presence of holiness. All those "fear of the Lord" passages in Scripture? The Hebrew word for "awe" is usually translated as "fear." Note, too, "the fear of the LORD is the beginning of wisdom" (Ps 111:10).

Throughout Scripture in all traditions, mere mortals report shaking in their flip-flops at a glimpse of the Divine. Angels never reveal themselves as such without first announcing, "Fear not," because they're awesome, in the true meaning of that word.

Feeling fearful? Perhaps you're resisting change or you're about to be visited by an angel.

Alas, your spiritual growth will stay somewhat stalled unless and until you become open to seeing and doing things differently. Willingness, then, is an essential practice for Seekers that's ongoing and never-ending—something else you might need to muster some willingness to accept. It's also a radical practice, the taproot from which every other practice is nourished. Plan on recommitting to the practice of willingness whenever resistance shows up, and it will show up, usually but not exclusively during times of life cycle transition.

Manifestations of unwillingness range from artful avoidance to elaborate denial.[2] It can show up as apathy or reluctance, rather than downright defiance.

You'll need to discover how you typically express unwillingness and learn what triggers it. You may need to better understand when saying "no" is an appropriate and important way to maintain healthy boundaries[3] and when it's not that at all, but an impediment to developing empathy (see Chapter 7: Empathy). These are psychosocial issues that, when left unexamined, will make spiritual development difficult, if not near-completely impossible.

Now that you've landed in the domain of developmental and cognitive psychology, you may need to muster the willingness to work with a psychotherapist. Or, be willing to work with a new therapist, preferably one who appreciates the relationship between psychology and spirituality, as well as the impact institutionalized religion has on both.

Let's Go Shopping . . . for a Psychotherapist!

Finding a good psychotherapist can be quite the challenge, especially if you must have costs covered by health insurance. Finding someone who is well trained, experienced, and licensed is the least of it. Plan to have a phone or in-person consult to explore your compatibility.

Depending on your issues and cognitive style, some modalities will be more (or less) effective than others. Look for and ask about the following when you go shopping for a therapist:

- *Approach:* Will you start with issues and behaviors here and now? Will you focus almost exclusively on your childhood? Will you explore your entire family system or just your parents?

- *Style:* Will you do all the talking? Will the therapist offer feedback, suggestions for behavior change, assignments to stay focused in between sessions?

- *Duration:* Will you get through issues in weekly sessions over a period of months? Must you commit to three to five sessions a week for years? Something in-between?

- *Medication:* Will medication be viewed as a first or maybe or last resort? If the therapist is a psychologist or social worker, does she or he work with someone trained in psychiatry or psychopharmacology who can prescribe medication?

Remember, too, that no matter how much you might want to forget a family or personal history of addiction, chronic illness, physical disability, or psychiatric disorder, your therapy will be much more effective if you work with someone experienced in these treatment areas.

Finally, if religion is or has been a major factor in your life, then seek and find a therapist who understands its impact.[4]

Yes, it's a lot of work, but remember: no willingness, no change; no change, no growth. You may experience connections with the Divine and get glimpses of the sacred, but these will remain as occasional flashes of light on the scrim of self until you're willing to deal with obstacles to spiritual growth, including whatever has made some or all of the traditional practices stop working for you.

Practice of . . .	Involves Willingness to . . .
Curiosity	explore the unknown, encounter mystery, ask questions, feel confused, be surprised
Empathy	feel pain, experience injustice, recognize suffering, show compassion
Generosity	give unconditionally, be forgiving, provide hospitality, trust divine providence
Delight	be amused, encounter absurdity, embrace irony, experience joy, express happiness

PRACTICING THE PRACTICE OF WILLINGNESS

Discover what's blocking your spiritual growth by creating a list of everything you're absolutely totally completely *unwilling* to change about your personality and your life, including your perceptions, beliefs, attitudes, and behavior.

After finishing this catalog of defiance, review each item and then ask and answer, "Why wouldn't I want to change this?" "How does refusing to change impede my spiritual growth?" While you're at it, take a look at how unwilling you are to defer gratification. Consciousness evolves over time, so if you stink at deferring gratification, you'll need to work on that, too. (Note: Revisit this after practicing curiosity for a while.)

Groove willingness into a habit for being by starting each of forty consecutive days[5] declaring, "For today I am willing to . . ." Use your list of stuff you're unwilling to change. Need more or other suggestions? How about starting with this: "I'm willing to be wrong about everything I thought I knew about religion and spiritual life."

Too much? How about: "I'm open to the possibility of being wrong about almost everything I thought I knew about religion and spiritual life."

Irony Alert: If you're willing to retool some traditional practices, try the following:

- Pray for willingness.

- Focus your *lectio divina* on Scripture having to do with willingness (to trust in God), starting with these go-to verses:

"Restore to me the joy of your salvation, / and sustain in me a willing spirit" (Ps 51:12).

"For surely I know the plans I have for you, says the LORD, plans for your welfare and not for harm, to give you a future with hope" (Jer 29:11).

"Trust in the LORD with all your heart, / and do not rely on your own insight" (Prov 3:5).

- Focus your nightly Examen[6] on willingness.

Is willingness still too much of a challenge? Not quite ready to practice this practice? Then back it up and be willing to become willing. This isn't just a clever play on words but one of many valuable tips for getting spiritually unstuck that I learned in the rooms of twelve-step recovery. To paraphrase Matthew 5:37, Let your "yes" be "yes," and your "no" be "maybe . . . at some point."

Willingness and the World of Twelve-Step Recovery

Willingness is so inherently key to recovery from addiction that in the main texts of Alcoholics Anonymous (i.e., the Big Book *Alcoholics Anonymous*, *Twelve Steps and Twelve Traditions*) "willingness" shows up 31 times, "willing" occurs 67 times, and an entire step (Step 6) focuses on the pesky business of becoming "entirely ready."[7]

Articulations of willingness include:
- "came to believe" (Step 2)
- "There is only one key, and it is called willingness . . ." (Step 3)
- "were entirely ready" (Step 6)
- "we became willing" (Step 8)

KNOW THYSELF—WILLINGNESS

Spiritual growth always involves change and the prospect of change scares the snot out of most people, even if they don't admit it. Resistance in its many forms looms large and becomes a barrier to practicing willingness. Start clearing all that out by asking:

- What or who made willingness seem dangerous?

- When and why did resistance become my go-to stance?

- How does my resistance typically manifest? As a physical feeling in the body? an emotional state? behavior?

Consider the Alternatives	
Willingness	
This . . .	*Or this . . .*
Open	Apathetic
Amenable	Averse
Cooperative	Disagreeable
Inclined	Opposed

Chapter 6

Curiosity

Not long after you learned how to say "no" you discovered another fabulously powerful one-syllable word: "why." It would be your best linguistic option until you could pile words into questions like, "What does that really mean?" and "How do you know that?" and "Did you just make that up?"

You asked about the existence and meaning of everything and while this phase of your development may have driven grown-ups nuts, it opened up your world. Incessant inquiry helped you make logical connections and, depending on the wisdom and honesty of whom you asked, enabled you to reject ones that weren't. Whatever you could see, hear, smell, touch, and taste was worth exploring until you discovered it wasn't.

Over time your curiosity got shut down, certainly not always and everywhere, but often enough by exhausted caregivers, overworked teachers, and besieged bosses who delivered this message: "Stop asking so many questions." Even if your natural curiosity wasn't completely quashed out of existence at school, church, or later on in the workplace, you learned how to assess where and when you could safely examine circumstances and poke at reality.

Along the way, you discovered where and when your squirm-worthy questions were "inappropriate" or would be "addressed later." As a result, not only did you stop asking because it was unsafe to ask, but you managed to mute the curiosity that generated those questions.

Maybe in the world of church you were plenty inquisitive until rhythms and routines of religious observance lulled you into complacency (see Chapter 4: Sorting Through Structure). You experienced a certain level of comfort in knowing that "we've always done it this way" but comfort has morphed into placid indifference.

If you sigh with happy relief at not having to do another thing when anyone says, "more will be revealed," and don't bother pushing back when told to "pray on it," then it's probably time to make curiosity your go-to practice.

As a Seeker, you have every right and soul-searching responsibility to ask about the why, when, and how of all creation. Spiritual life should support, not diminish, your commitment to curiosity and enthusiastic exploration. *Seeker* . . . get it?

Employed with intentionality and consciousness, curiosity becomes a spiritual practice that can:

- *Slow down reactivity.* Pausing or stopping entirely in the midst of turmoil to be curious will create time and space to calm down enough to be a witness to whatever is happening.

- *Open new gateways to wisdom and knowledge.* You're probably willing to admit what you don't know, but how about what you don't even know you don't know? Curiosity ushers you into—and eventually through—that cloud of cosmic unknowing.[1]

- *Generate enthusiasm for inquiry.* Goals shift when curiosity is the practice. Confusion becomes an opportunity for examination rather than clarification. Aggravation becomes an opportunity for exploration rather than resolution. The lack of definitive answers becomes an opportunity for passionate inquiry rather than frustration.

- *Substitute light for heat.* Heated emotions like anger and disgust tend to lose thermal intensity when explored rather than (or soon after being) acted out. Notice what happens to self-righteous outrage when its source is examined from a place of curiosity.

Detach . . . With Curiosity

Detachment is a core concept in twelve-step recovery programs for people involved with addicts, with that "involvement" ranging from family relations to less intimate yet often equally complex work and community relationships.

Participants in "-Anon" programs (e.g., Al-Anon) learn to reduce near-irresistible urges to manipulate, intervene, and fix. From the Al-Anon literature: "Detachment is neither kind nor unkind. It does not imply judgement or condemnation of the person or situation from which we are detaching." The point is to "detach with love," rather than storm off with disgust. Another option: detach with curiosity.

The whole world is a spiritual practice field and opportunities to practice curiosity abound. God's grace is always somewhere in the messiness of life, and asking increasingly pointed questions about what, where, when, why, and how will help you discover it. Become willing to opt for being curious the next time you feel bored, bothered, and bewildered.

Curiosity has an alchemical ability to restore gleam to spiritual disciplines that have become dulled by routinized use.

It can transform doubt and discontent into . . . well, who knows? You don't. Not yet and maybe not ever, but you're interested in finding out, which is why curiosity, like willingness, is an essential practice of being.

Curiosity Gone Bad

There's a downside to everything and curiosity is no exception. You can see curiosity going bad when friendly inquisitiveness turns into a barrage of inappropriate questions.

Snooping around and meddling is also evidence of curiosity gone bad. Being oblivious to signs and signals to back off or stop completely is not proof of fearless curiosity but weak boundaries.

Such suboptimal behavior is always easier to observe in others. You'll have a better chance of observing and stopping your own curiosity from going bad by examining your motivation for putting curiosity into action so intrusively.

PRACTICING THE PRACTICE OF CURIOSITY

Recognize the sure signs of ennui, especially during traditional practice. Boredom might manifest physically by yawning or fidgeting or both. It may show up cognitively as not being able to follow or repeat what you're supposed to be following or repeating. Your mind wanders and doesn't return until the final "Amen."

Treat these signs as your cue to get fascinated by whatever causes you to check out. Be curious about body-mind connects or disconnects. Go meta-level and get curious about boredom itself. And do not stifle a yawn; it's a sign your brain is too warm and you need to cool it down to perk yourself up.[2]

Generate a list of what you absolutely know and believe about spiritual life. Now become super-interested in how you acquired this absolute knowledge and belief. At what age and stage of life were you taught about connecting with something greater and beyond yourself? In what setting did you learn your deeply held beliefs and truths? How were you taught (e.g., memorization, repetition) and who did the teaching? After exploring these questions, reexamine your list. Anything you now need to remove? Anything you need to add? If not, allow yourself to wander through wondering about what won't—or can't—change.

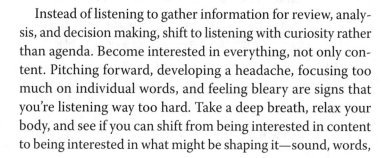

Pay attention to all instances of serendipity, coincidence, congruence, happenchance—or anything else that seems to fall into place without easy explanation. Even if you already believe there's no such thing as "coincidence," consciously use these moments to contemplate how the invisible hand of God is being made visible. Get curious about why these things might be happening at that particular moment or time in your life.

Instead of listening to gather information for review, analysis, and decision making, shift to listening with curiosity rather than agenda. Become interested in everything, not only content. Pitching forward, developing a headache, focusing too much on individual words, and feeling bleary are signs that you're listening way too hard. Take a deep breath, relax your body, and see if you can shift from being interested in content to being interested in what might be shaping it—sound, words, tone, facial expressions, body language. You're no longer listening "to" but listening "for." For what? You don't yet know. You're practicing curiosity.

"It's a Mystery"

In the world of faith, there's a long tradition of idiomatic expressions that get trotted out as code for, "Shut *up* about it already." Not always, but often enough to squelch curiosity under the guise of providing spiritual guidance. Note, too, how some of these secular verbal panaceas have pervaded the language of faith:

- It's a mystery.
- Lift it up.
- It's all good.
- Put it at the foot of the cross.
- God has a plan.
- It is what it is.

KNOW THYSELF—CURIOSITY

Social institutions, including but not limited to religion, have played some kind of role in diminishing your curiosity. Discover just how and for how long your sense of wonder and passion for exploration have been thwarted by asking:

- When was I most curious about my surroundings? What captured my curiosity the most—people, places, things, cats?

- Which traditional practices seem to best encourage and support curiosity?

- How and when has my spiritual curiosity been best nurtured?

Consider the Alternatives	
Curiosity	
This . . .	*Or this . . .*
Exploring	Complacent
Fascinated	Disinterested
Inquisitive	Bored
Interested	Indifferent

Chapter 7

Empathy

Of course you're compassionate; you're a Seeker for crying out loud. You know the Divine is fully present in all things; we're all connected and beloved creations of God. Your heart aches for the hungry and homeless. You feel called to serve others with grace and generosity.

Except, you *do* tend to wonder about that sacred interconnectedness whenever you step into whatever the cat horked up while you were blissfully meditating. Also, when an obviously too-old-to-drive person slows down traffic. Oneness with that? No thank you.

No aching heart for the neighbor whose front lawn is widely considered a disgrace. Major heartache while watching video clips of refugee crises in remote countries. Occasional heartache—or is it heartburn?—while scrolling through the "outrage fêtes" on social media. Mostly you're numbed by the ever-present outward and visible signs of suffering. You'll get around to feeling the world's pain and grief, but not right now. Maybe later.

Does any of this seem at all familiar? If so, it's time to focus on empathy[1] as a spiritual practice, even if you collect Sacred Heart of Jesus images and can recite Buddhist metta meditation without looking up the sequence.[2]

Empathy is a practice that requires the willingness to identify, acknowledge, and explore nuanced feelings beyond "happy, sad, mad, and glad."[3] As a result, empathy is a spiritual practice that will:

- reveal connections obscured by social demographics (no longer are male or female, rich or poor, educated or illiterate separated by circumstances; we are all one in grief, loneliness, despair, and fear [Gal 3:28]);

- disclose how feelings have shaped and perhaps over-determined your attitudes and responses (you want to acknowledge the past, not stay stuck in feelings about it);

- compel you to sort fact from horror fiction (emotional intensity is not proof of reality but usually a signal to do some fact-checking; feelings are not facts, no matter how real they seem);

- provide yet another opportunity to debride and heal emotional wounds (you cannot heal what you cannot feel);[4] and

- enhance your ability to be compassionate (the literal *translation* of compassion is to "suffer with" while "to help alleviate" is the common definition of compassion; you can do good things [see Chapter 8: Generosity], but that doesn't automatically make you compassionate).

Coming to Terms with More Terms

Dig into the research on compassion and you'll swiftly discover that "sympathy" and "empathy" are terms used in distinct ways by everyone working in this rapidly growing field of study and practice.[5]

When it comes to spiritual growth, these are distinctions that really do make a difference.

At the broadest level, the distinction is based on (1) how someone arrives at understanding another's experience; and (2) how someone responds as a result of that understanding.[6]

Sympathy: Recognizing misfortune/suffering and then feeling sorrow at best, pity at worst. *Based on:* hearing enough stories, observing enough situations, and watching enough ripped-from-the-headlines-made-for-TV movies to have a better-than-average clue about what others might be feeling, not actually having #all-thefeels[7] except, perhaps, relief. *Sympathy example:* Buying a condolence card and maybe getting around to sending it.

Empathy: Recognizing misfortune/suffering and then truly feeling what someone else is feeling. *Based on:* having the same or substantively similar experience and an ability to feel. *Compassion example:* Expressing concern and, based on shared experience, providing what someone else might need.

Feelings . . . oh, oh, whoa . . . feelings. I could be projecting, but even longtime Seekers will reflexively cringe at the suggestion of exploring feelings, get a little too excited about getting back "in touch" with them, or some combination of these reactions.

Complex dicey things, feelings. Empathy will be a challenging practice if you were raised in a home where having feelings and emotional responses, let alone discussing them, was verboten. *Stop crying! Our business is no one else's beeswax!*

Empathy will be a challenging practice if you were raised in a religious tradition where all suffering, no matter how debilitating, was characterized as redemptive. *Behold The Cross! You think you have it bad?*

It's easy to get flummoxed by feelings and the meanings you may have unconsciously ascribed to them. Feelings are multilayered shape-shifting things and it's a psychoanalytic given that the primary feeling is more topsoil than bedrock. Dig into the anger and discover disappointment; dig deeper through the disappointment and discover grief. Dig into the indignation and discover vulnerability; dig deeper through the vulnerability and discover fear.

But Seekers welcome challenges, so it's another round of "Inward ho" because empathy is a prerequisite for authentic compassion. And don't take this in a blamey-shamey way, but since empathy is considered one of the five key components of emotional intelligence (EQ),[8] consciously practicing it should (*should!*) be on your spiritual to-do list. But here's some good news: empathy is an emotional skill that can be "taught and caught,"[9] although there are abundant arguments for every possible assertion about whether it's a fixed personality trait or a choice.[10]

Motive and Motivation

Pay attention to intention and watch out for doing your healing at the expense of others. Being able to say "been there, survived that" can help both giver and recipient, but be super-careful about diving into one-to-one anything without first considering the psychological impact on you.

While it may seem only logical—and certainly empathy-driven—to serve the homeless if you've been homeless, counsel battered women if you've been one, or to volunteer at your local hospice if you've watched a loved one die without dignity, you may not be emotionally ready.

Even if you believe you've done better than survived trauma, proceed with caution. Your survival is not proof that you'll be able to alleviate another person's suffering without becoming rewounded, perhaps significantly.

Ah, the never-ending process of self-examination and healing. Does it ever end? Not in this lifetime and certainly not for Seekers. For us, everything is always under construction. You know what this means, right? You may need to sign on for another stint of psychotherapeutic work to reevaluate your track record for establishing and maintaining healthy emotional boundaries. You may also need to spend time at the intersection of behavioral psychology and spirituality to discover if spiritual bypass has become your default defense against feeling too much or too deeply.

Spiritual Bypassing

Of all the concepts emerging from the self-discovery movement of the mid-1980s through mid-1990s, spiritual bypassing has to be among the most valuable.

As defined by psychologist John Welwood, spiritual bypassing is a defense mechanism in which spiritual rationales are invoked to avoid dealing with unexamined and unresolved issues.[11] Psychologist Robert Augustus Masters has characterized it as "avoidance in holy drag."[12]

Spiritual bypassing behavior hides in plain sight among well-intentioned Seekers as well as those in the religion biz (e.g., clergy, religious, lay ministers).

It's difficult to identify because it sounds so . . . spiritual: "I'm suffering, so my spiritual practices must be working."

"God and the angels protect me." "I eat to stay grounded in the presence of so much human suffering." "I'm not 'isolating,' I'm observing sacred solitude." It also manifests as premature forgiveness, anger avoidance, extreme deference (especially to religious authorities and spiritual teachers), and excessive niceness—and this is the short list!

Doing any of this stuff? Good news: it could just be a phase of spiritual development. Other news: you might benefit from working with a therapist with training and experience in transpersonal psychology.

You'll need to explore self to go beyond self, be willing to see and feel your own brokenness before being able to recognize it in others, be willing to view your own pain and suffering as a gift.[13] Empathy is a practice of being that will help you shift from *feeling for* to *feeling with* in a healthy way that might not feel especially terrific, but will reveal what you already know—that the Divine is fully present in all of it.

Is It Caring . . .

- You pause and assess situations before diving in to help.
- You offer superb advice without being deeply invested in it being taken.
- You feel whole when being compassionate, even if no one expresses appreciation.

. . . Or Is It Codependency?

- You're a little too quick to help, even when no one asks for it.
- You're delighted when others depend upon your involvement.
- Your sense of accomplishment is tied to other people's appreciation.

Compassion Fatigue

Good news: your empathy has led you to compassionate action.

Bad news: your compassionate action may end up producing what's officially known as Compassion Fatigue.[14]

Compassion Fatigue (a.k.a., secondary traumatic stress) is the more recognized term for what happens when ongoing and consistent contact with situations requiring compassion ends up significantly eroding it. You don't have to be a professional caregiver to experience Compassion Fatigue.

How will you know this is creeping up on you? Notice when you start feeling hopeless, powerless, depressed, apathetic, anxious, and that no one gives a rat's ass about what you're doing to relieve anyone else's suffering. If you excel at ignoring feelings, then notice if you develop headaches, dizziness, difficulty breathing, a rapid heartbeat, or have trouble sleeping.

While these are also physical symptoms of burnout, that's classified as a different condition (see Chapter 10: Spiritual Practice Burnout) because it's due to overwork, not trauma.

PRACTICING THE PRACTICE OF EMPATHY

Assess your current capacity for empathy by taking a few of the self-assessment tests available online, starting with Baron-Cohen's well-known Empathy Quotient (EQ) test, either the full 60-question or 40-item version.[15] After that, complete Davis's Interpersonal Reactivity Index, a 28-item questionnaire that has become somewhat more preferred among clinicians because it assesses four different facets of empathy.[16] Since empathy includes being able to read nonverbal cues, check out the Reading the Mind in the Eyes test, another assessment created by Baron-Cohen.[17]

Review the results and, especially if you feel less-than-thrilled with your test scores, contemplate your:

- *Willingness:* Since empathy involves the ability to recognize feelings, how willing are you to do the work—or yet more work—to explore the breadth and depth of yours?

- *Curiosity:* Some people seem to be better than others at recognizing and expressing nuanced feelings. Why do you suppose some test questions seemed easy to answer and others not so much?

- *Generosity:* Take this Self-Compassion Test[18] to help determine whether you're being too tough on yourself . . . again.

- *Delight:* How might you delight in this perhaps unexpected invitation to cultivate greater awareness of your feelings and emotions? Not delighted? Loop back through the other practices of being.

Your body provides lots of useful information about empathy if you explore how and where you feel it physically. It's relatively easy to label something as suffering when weeping is involved, but that's not the only way distress shows up in the body.

Notice how you feel physically when you're feeling emotional distress. How about when you're in the presence of someone else's suffering? Where in your body do you feel anger, grief, hurt, worry, or fear? What do emotions feel like physically? What happens to your ability to breathe? your muscles? your heartbeat? (see Appendix B: Spiritual Survival Skills: The Body Scan).

While it's true that persistent migraines, indigestion, sore throats, and backaches might be due to something biochemical or structural, consider the possibility that your body might be revealing what your mind has yet to fully grasp.[19]

Learn how to recognize discomfort and distress in its many and often subtle physical manifestations so you can use them first for your own edification and protection and then to provide support to someone else.

Everyone has a story with real events and experiences that have changed them forever. Develop empathy for their story by exploring yours, and then compassionately listening to theirs.

Explore your own story: Make time to write your responses to these prompts: Which experiences have significantly shaped how you perceive the world around you and your feelings about being alive? What happened? What didn't happen? What needed to happen? What do you wish had happened? How has the truth of what happened changed over time? How has the quality of your storytelling changed over time?

Compassionately listen to someone else's story: Practice asking to hear someone else's story and then committing to listening without interruption. Practice saying, "Something like that happened to me . . ." and then waiting for an invitation to share your story, resisting every temptation to share if that invite isn't ever extended.

Speaker's meetings for twelve-step recovery groups, which are typically open to the public, provide extraordinary opportunities to hear stories being told with no agenda other than getting and staying honest. Twelve-step recovery program meetings also provide opportunities to witness what becomes possible when no "cross-talk" is allowed.

The source of your pain is likely to also be the source of someone else's. In what might seem like a weird version of metta meditation, contemplate commonalities:

- What pain and suffering do I feel?

- What pain and suffering might my loved ones feel?

- What pain and suffering might my most annoying coworker feel?

- What pain and suffering might all people feel?

KNOW THYSELF—EMPATHY

You've always thought of yourself as an empathetic person, but now you're realizing that maybe you're not . . . or not yet. Explore where you are on the transition from sympathy to empathy by asking:

- What typically slows me down or prevents me entirely from moving from sympathy to empathy?

- How do I know when I'm feeling empathy?

- What will I need to work on changing about myself to cultivate empathy?

Consider the Alternatives	
Empathy	
This . . .	*Or this . . .*
Identification	Indifference
Caring	Disregard
Sensitivity	Inattentiveness
Understanding	Thoughtlessness

Chapter 8

Generosity

Among all the spiritual practices of being, generosity is probably the easiest to grasp on every conceptual and practical level. You don't have to be raised in any particular religion to aspire to greater kindness, hospitality, or other forms of altruism that are considered baseline human decency. In the United States, volunteer work and charitable giving have always been part of the secular genome.

Plus, it doesn't take much religion education to know that generosity is a moral imperative within the Judeo-Christian tradition.

If you've done hard time in Sunday School or taken a college course in comparative religion, you (please, dear God) probably know that among Jews, generosity is synonymous with righteousness (*tzedakah*). Hebrew Scripture is filled with examples of God's mercy—with and without human pleas for forgiveness; stories about hospitality to strangers (e.g., Gen 18:1-10) and cautionary tales about being greedy and stingy (e.g., Ezek 16:49). Hundreds of commandments and guidelines, including ones about caring for the poor, kindness to aliens, and repentance appear throughout Torah—especially in Leviticus, Numbers, and Deuteronomy, where you'll also find rules for tithing (Deut 14:22-29).[1]

Moses Maimonides's Eight Degrees of Tzedakah

During the twelfth century, Sephardic Rabbi Moses Maimonides (Rambam) compiled all extant Jewish oral tradition, legal practices, rituals, and customs, in addition to centuries of rabbinic commentaries, debates, and rulings, into a ginormous encyclopedia. He also made pithy observations about *tzedakah* (translation: righteousness but often used colloquially to mean charitable giving).

According to Maimonides, the eight degrees of righteousness in the form of giving are incremental. Each stage represents a deeper level of consciousness about the act and impact of giving. At which level do you tend to live out your generosity?

1. To give grudgingly, reluctantly, or with regret;
2. To give less than one should, but with grace;
3. To give what one should, but only after being asked;
4. To give before one is asked;
5. To give without knowing who will receive it, although the recipient knows the identity of the giver;
6. To give without making known one's identity;
7. To give so that neither giver nor recipient knows the identity of the others;
8. To help another to become self-supporting by means of a gift, a loan, or by finding employment for the one in need.

In Christian Scripture, reaching out to the lost, the last, and the least to fulfill the greatest commandment to love God is pretty much the point of all gospel stories and teachings (Matt 22:34-40; 25:42-45). The relationship between generosity and faith, underscored over and over again in letters from leaders of the early church, would eventually give rise to a theological grudge match about criteria for salvation, but don't let that obscure its central importance.

By the thirteenth century, the acts of compassionate generosity Jesus preached would be formalized by St. Thomas Aquinas as the corporal and spiritual works of mercy. For Christians, generosity with stuff and spirit is the Gospel-in-practice. Sometimes this is generated by empathy, but more typically a matter of recognizing and then believing in God's grace and divine providence—do/give unto others.

Given this rich history, appearing here in truncated form, you'd think generosity would be a no-sweat, no-brainer practice for Seekers, but really it isn't. Oh, the human condition. Who among us hasn't been withholding, miserly, and mean on occasion . . . or more frequently.

Not you?

Well, how about those times you averted your eyes to avoid dealing with the homeless while stopped at a red traffic light? Or when you just couldn't muster the energy to let anyone camp out in your guest room for an indeterminate amount of time? When was the last time you let someone have the bigger half or last slice of something you really wanted to eat when you were hungry? Or the last time you granted someone an emotional free pass for being late or a complete no-show? What's that, you've never been mean? So I guess you never attended middle school. Wait, was that me being mean?

Let's get real. Some forms of generosity are easier to practice than others. In fact, most people really are generous with stuff like food, clothing, shelter, and money. It's easy to offer and then follow through with home-based hospitality when your guests are friends. Tithing is tolerable when monies are automatically transferred from your bank account to the recipient institution.

Our much bigger challenge is noticing stinginess of spirit. Being welcoming, encouraging, appreciative, comforting, kind, and forgiving is psychospiritually tougher than dumping out-of-style clothing into a roadside collection bin. Yes, it's possible to be generous with stuff and miserly in spirit.

What gets in the way is, of course, the usual human weirdness: dodgy motives, unmet emotional needs, way too permeable personal boundaries, fear of either not having enough or giving too much away at one's own expense. But thanks to all the work you've done and continue to do, you know enough to heed these little canaries chirping away in the mineshaft of your consciousness. It's time to practice generosity when you notice—or someone so generously points out—these attitudes and behaviors:

- *Lots of complaining.* Some grousing is an acceptable way to let off steam, but you're doing something else. Could be new behavior, could be old predictable behavior. In any case, you complain about nearly everyone and everything much of the time. You see absolutely no or precious little evidence of God's grace in the world, certainly not in other people. Possible exception: videos of kittens and puppies playing, but why aren't there more of those? Time for a gratitude adjustment.[2]

- *Emotional clutching onto and/or physical hoarding.* Nothing wrong with taking care of self and loved ones. As the flight attendants say, "put the oxygen mask on your own face first." You, however, are reducing everyone's oxygen intake with fear-based emotional smothering and micromanaging. Alternatively or in addition to that, you hang onto possessions and stash away money so there will be enough. Time to check out that paradox about giving and receiving.[3]

- *Becoming exceedingly reluctant to apologize.* Of course you're guilty of bad behavior, but everyone else's is so much worse. They, in fact, should be apologizing to you. Time to brush up on the spiritual reasons for and psychological benefits of forgiveness, as well as the process of repentance. Maybe also revisit the prayer attributed to St. Francis of Assisi, especially the "where there is injury, pardon" and "it is in pardoning that we are pardoned" parts.[4]

Corporal and Spiritual Works of Mercy

We have St. Thomas Aquinas to thank for organizing Gospel imperatives into what's commonly referred to (by Catholics) as the corporal and spiritual works of mercy.

Material and physical generosity:

- feed the hungry
- shelter the homeless
- clothe the naked
- visit the sick and imprisoned
- bury the dead
- give alms to the poor

Emotional and spiritual generosity:

- instruct
- advise
- console
- comfort
- forgive
- bear wrongs patiently

You'd think living in a secular environment wherein generosity is esteemed would make this a relatively easy practice. Well, it is and it isn't.

Knowing what generally qualifies as generosity makes the practice easy. Dealing with what gets in the way, especially when it comes to generosity of spirit, requires consciousness and effort.

It's a challenge worth taking on because practicing generosity will help you move beyond self to become a person for others, engaged with the world and part of a greater sacred whole. If that doesn't seem to be happening fast enough, then you probably need to fling some encouragement, comfort, kindness, and acceptance in your own direction. Maybe also some cash to buy chocolate.

PRACTICING THE PRACTICE OF GENEROSITY

Assess your current practice of generosity by listing how you're already generous with stuff and spirit. Write all this out so it's easier to scrutinize. Next, review each item and ponder your:

- *Willingness:* To what extent has your generosity been determined by obligation? How willing are you to be generous without external structure and support, or mechanisms for accountability?

- *Curiosity:* How important is it for you to know specifics about recipients and the impact of your generosity? If this turns out to be very important, become willing to explore why.

- *Empathy:* To what extent is your generosity driven by your experiences? Do you truly empathize with conditions or go directly to being generous because it's easier than feeling all the feelings?

- *Delight:* How has your generosity generated delight and how does that manifest?

After contemplating all this, what should you probably add to this list? What practices of being—willingness, curiosity, empathy, delight—could use more . . . practice?

Generosity doesn't need to be embedded in an official event with a crowdfunding site, Facebook page and Pinterest board, or with badges and T-shirts. Mundane ways to practice generosity of stuff and spirit include the following:

- Support friends and neighbors by providing food, child care, pet sitting, household repairs, or yard work.

- Be an angel in retail hell by reshelving your unwanted items, letting elders go ahead of you at checkout, bagging someone else's groceries, and walking your own damn shopping cart to the return rack.

- Encourage others with pep notes posted to social media, or go crazy-wild and send them via snail mail.

- Offer up your precious seat on public transportation to someone else.

- Send $15 to the charity that sent the personalized mailing labels with no cost or obligation, especially if you use them.

- Usher others into the flow of traffic with a gentle wave of your hand, rather than the flip of your finger.

Practice generosity of spirit by giving others the benefit of the doubt. Unless their behavior is habitual to the point of being destructive or dangerous, forgive them for:

- what might seem to be gossiping or trash-talking others—or you;

- arriving late to a public gathering or personal get-together;

- forgetting to express acknowledgment or appreciation;

- not apologizing for insensitivity or flat-out bad behavior;

- being oblivious to circumstances and situations around them;

- dramatic self-absorption, angry outbursts, and weep-a-thons; and

- things they might not even know they are—or are not—doing.[5]

Reexamine not only your willingness to forgive, but also how you go about seeking forgiveness from others. Saying "I'm sorry" is not enough and may, given how swiftly people seem to apologize these days, be perceived as expedient rather than authentic. Enhance the credibility—and rigor—of your apologies by:

- recognizing the wrongdoing and being able to articulate it;

- becoming clear about the impact of your behavior on others, as well as on your own secular and spiritual health;

- committing to changing attitudes and behavior;

- not repeating the offense, especially when facing the same or similar situations;

- making restitution;

- counterbalancing bad behavior with good deeds; and

- sustaining attitudinal and behavioral change over time.

Wash, rinse, repeat as necessary.

KNOW THYSELF—GENEROSITY

That's right, you believe you're a generous person who easily and consistently practices generosity. As a Seeker at any stage of spiritual development, you probably really and truly are all that. Yet, there's no harm and possibly some illuminating benefit in taking another look by asking:

- When and how do circumstances determine my level and type of generosity?

- Which acts of generosity or kindness—as recipient or giver—have meant the most to me? What made these gestures so meaningful and memorable?

- What do I let get in the way of giving to others whatever was so generously given to me?

Consider the Alternatives	
Generosity	
This . . .	*Or this . . .*
Altruistic	Stingy
Big-hearted	Mean-spirited
Giving	Withholding
Hospitable	Begrudging

Chapter 9

Delight

"Rejoice always, . . . give thanks in all circumstances . . ." (1 Thess 5:16-18).

Rejoice . . . *always*? Seems a bit extreme, plus an over-the-top invitation to exhaustion. And isn't always, like never, one of those hyperbolic words that should always never be used for anything ever?

Give thanks in . . . *all* circumstances? Also a bit much, although probably not for Seekers who welcome (almost) all opportunities to learn, grow, and use "journal" as a verb. As a Seeker, you already appreciate how the most unexpected spiritual growth nearly always[1] results from facing rather than avoiding difficult circumstances. Nevertheless, giving thanks is tough when situations aren't anything you'd ever want or choose.

Delight is the spiritual practice of being that will help you give thanks in suboptimal circumstances and count it all joy—with or without throwing a big party with a chocolate fountain.

Delight!

Such a frothy confection of a word, almost onomatopoetic in the way it sparkles. And, so versatile. At one end of the spectrum, delight is bundled up in a quiet and cozy sense of wonder; at the other, it bursts forth from the confines of socialized self as spontaneous laughter or song or dance.

Delight is a deeper happiness and a more expansive sense of joy, a punctuation mark for curiosity, a possible by-product of optimism and not at all contingent on having fun. It's amplified by unexpected pleasures, like the Christmas cactus that blooms on Easter. It's stoked by encounters with ironic weirdness, like seeing the dog dressed all matchy-matchy with its human. Grim has a chance of turning to gratitude when delight is practiced with attention to intention.[2] And while it might not always seem obvious as such, delight is a spiritual imperative within the Judeo-Christian religious tradition.

The ancient Israelites so understood the importance of delight that it shows up throughout Hebrew Scripture as an essential way to serve God.[3] It's even codified as days set aside as "appointed feasts of the Lord"[4] for grateful rejoicing and happiness. Delight is expressed in stories like the one about Sarah's joyful laughter in response to Isaac's miraculous birth (Gen 21:6)[5] and the exuberant dance and song Miriam leads after the Israelites safely flee Egyptian slavery (Exod 15:20-21).

Verses about the gift of joy appear throughout the writings (Ketuvim), which include Psalms, Proverbs, Ecclesiastes, and Nehemiah. In song after song, the psalmist invites the righteous to rejoice in the Lord, to be jubilant with joy, to shout and sing with joy, to worship with gladness (e.g., Ps 32:11; 66:1-2; 68:3; 95:2; 100:1-2). Joy plus wisdom and knowledge are bestowed upon the righteous (e.g., Prov 21:15; Eccl 2:26; 5:19-20). Joy of the Lord provides strength (Neh 8:10), and millennia before modern medicine, King Solomon recognized the salutary benefits of a cheerful heart (Prov 17:22).

Healing Laughter

Reader's Digest had been including reader-submitted jokes on its "Laughter, the Best Medicine" page for nearly fifty years before Norman Cousins landed an article in the *New England Journal of Medicine* making exactly this point. The idea that laughter could have therapeutic value became even more popularized when Cousins published his book *Anatomy of an Illness* in 1979.[6]

There's never been much quibbling about the positive psychological benefits of laughter, but still the medical community spent nearly two decades being cautious about making similar claims about laughter's physiological benefits.

This finally changed when clinical evidence emerged to support anecdotal evidence about laughter's positive impact on cardiovascular, central nervous, endocrine, immune, muscular, and respiratory systems.[7]

These days laughter and humor are routinely characterized as "therapeutic allies" in the healing process, which is a more buttoned-down way of noting this spiritual wisdom from sometime between the tenth and third centuries BCE: "A cheerful heart is a good medicine . . ." (Prov 17:22).

And then there's Christian Scripture, where you don't have to be a biblical scholar to notice changes in the tone and context for how joy is articulated. References to delight are nearly nonexistent and verses are primarily reminders to rejoice and be glad about salvation (e.g., Matt 5:12; Luke 6:23). Also, as assurances that pain and suffering will eventually morph into joy (e.g., John 16:20, 22; Acts 5:40-42; Jas 1:2; 1 Pet 1:6-9).

Dancing appears twice in the Synoptic Gospels; neither are exemplars of delight. In one reference, a dance at Herod's birthday banquet does not go well for John the Baptist (Mark 6:14-29). In the other, an elder son has a jealous hissy fit when

the wayward son's return is celebrated with feasting and dancing (Luke 15:11-32).

Nor do you have to study Christianity very rigorously to
know that at various points during its history joy has been
negatively equated with body-based pleasure-seeking despite
(or because of?) the erotic descriptions of devotion delivered
by the mystic saints.[8] Look through the lens of delight as you
review the history of sacred art, architecture, and sanctuary
décor. Blah blah blah . . . idolatry . . . but maybe also statues,
icons, stained glass windows, and the like were just way too
delightful? These days, thank God, there's plenty of evidence
in art, music, and poetry[9] to suggest joy is being restored to
its divinely appointed place—for some.

Anyways, as a Seeker, you already believe that "joy is the
most infallible sign of the presence of God."[10] You've lived
long enough to know dawn follows darkness, sorrow inevi-
tably gives way to joy, albeit not always swiftly enough (see
Chapter 1: About That Spiritual Journey). On a good day of
spiritual attainment, you're delighted to know that the end
of the journey is the beginning of something else that you're
willing to discover.

If you're working a twelve-step program of recovery, you're
increasingly "sure that God wants us to be happy, joyous, and
free."[11] If you're a fan of St. Teresa of Ávila, you've adopted
this declaration of hers as your personal prayer: "God save us
from sullen saints." You were delighted when, during his 2014
Christmas speech to the Roman Curia, Pope Francis included
the "disease of the funeral face" in his list of fifteen "diseases"
or "temptations."[12]

Still, to practice delight within and beyond the confines of
church-the-building, you may need to:

- *Reexamine how you've connected pleasure and shame.*
  Have you been taught to consider anything pleasurable

as self-indulgent, wrong, sinful, or shameful? How about pleasure derived from anything involving the senses or . . . your body?!? Think you've moved beyond all that? Maybe you have, but maybe you haven't . . . not really. Delight isn't pleasure sanitized; it's pleasure distilled to divine essence.

- *Reconsider how you connect feeling delight with having fun.* What do you think is—or believe should be—the connection between having fun and feeling delight? Reality check: Do you truly feel authentic deep happiness when you do so-called "fun" things? While you're at it, ponder how surprise factors in to how you define fun or delight.

- *Clean up addictions.* Do you use alcohol or substances for a jolt of joy or to enhance pleasure? How about doing things that are categorized as "process" (i.e., behavioral v. physiological) addictions?[13]

The Shadow Side of Delight

It's difficult to separate sensory stimulation and delight, nor should you unless something else starts happening. That "something else" is a shift in attitude from "how lovely to feel" to "absolutely must feel" and from "that would be nice" to "must have."

Welcome to the shadow side of delight, which becomes especially visible when attitude drives behavior.

There's a difference between capturing moments of delight and being held captive by it. Key signs and symptoms include some or all of the following:

- confusing pleasure with relief from something else (e.g., fear or pain);
- uncontrollable drive to stoke and experience pleasure;

- inability to stop pleasure-producing behavior despite negative results (e.g., interfering with normal daily functioning);
- spiritual bypassing by rationalizing pursuit of pleasure as "divine bliss" or "sacred ecstasy."

Practicing this practice of being involves exploring whatever diminishes, blocks, or may completely obliterate delight, and then healing whatever needs to be healed to encounter and recognize it. As Seekers, we've made a commitment to not only discover and experience the delight of Divine Presence, but to reveal it to others as well. How delightful is that?

PRACTICING THE PRACTICE OF DELIGHT

To practice delight, you need to recognize it and creating a Delight List will help. Create a Delight List by listing at least twenty people, places, things, situations, and events that are sources of true delight. These can be categorical (e.g., kittens, anything purple, all-you-can-eat buffets) as well as specific (e.g., a whiff of vanilla, local duck pond, watching ants drag ginormous crumbs). Include physical as well as psychological sources of delight. Include the obvious and obscure, the sincere and ironic. Remember to add things that generated delight once upon a time, and then practice curiosity to explore when and why that stopped.

Yes, at least twenty items. Committing to generating these many sources of delight will help you think more expansively and creatively about where to discover—and recover—them. Write out this list to help imprint your insights at the cellular level.

Return to this list whenever you feel gloomy. Better yet, actively seek out items on this list when you start feeling disgruntled; don't wait until you've become mired in grim. Commit to using what you know about your personal sources of delight to actively seek it.

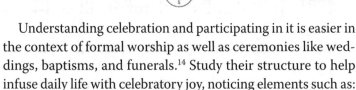

Practice exclaiming, "How delightful!" until that becomes an automatic way of perceiving your surroundings—chosen and unchosen. Relative to the latter, consider treating people, places, and things that aren't especially delightful as cues to consider how you could restore delight. If you practice centering prayer, make "delight" your sacred word for a season.

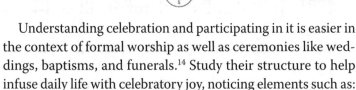

Understanding celebration and participating in it is easier in the context of formal worship as well as ceremonies like weddings, baptisms, and funerals.[14] Study their structure to help infuse daily life with celebratory joy, noticing elements such as:

- *Timing and sequence:* When are components introduced? When are new actions added? Does something need to be completed before something else begins? What happens if and when festive elements overlap?

- *Food and drink:* What role(s) do food and drink play in celebration? How are they included? When and how could they be (perhaps better) shared? How can the delight of food and drink be sustained while also respecting food allergies/sensitivities and an essential need to avoid alcohol?

- *Music:* How does music influence, if not shape, the celebratory nature of events? What types of music need to play in the background? When should music move to the foreground? When and how should music shift from passive listening to active participation?

What else would an exuberant celebration include? What would a quiet celebration involve? What would maximize delight for celebrants? What typically transforms an event from dull to delightful?

Build your appreciation of and capacity for delight by stimulating it in time-tested-and-proven ways:

- *Nature*: Walks, hikes, leisurely strolls through parks and nature preserves, or along a shoreline; stopping at a mountain overlook; signing up for an outdoor adventure with a naturalist, horticulturalist, geologist, or anyone who can help you see and then appreciate what you see. Physically unable to do that? Online technology provides work-arounds. Yes, "teletourism" is a thing![15]

- *Creativity*: Explore the arts and not just as an observer. Reality check: you don't need formal training to create art, make music, or dance. If the thought of creating art, dance, or music seems more terrifying than transcendent, you'll need to change your "I can't" mindset.[16] Alternatively, you could simply begin by doodling, dancing, or singing about and to the sacred in the privacy of your own home sanctuary.

- *Sensory stimulation*: Seek out opportunities to smell, see, and touch things that stimulate delight. Sniff essential oils, incense, candles. Which scents are delightfully delicious? Look at color swatches at a paint store.

Which colors delight? Is it time to repaint something in your home or office? Visit a fabric shop and touch different types of cloth. Which textures delight? There's a reason why satin and velvet are often characterized as "simply divine." Time to drape something, someone, or yourself in either—or both—of those fabrics?

KNOW THYSELF—DELIGHT

Elated, gladdened, jubilant, overjoyed . . . and you've never devoted a whole lot of time considering these synonyms for "delight" or if their nuanced meanings have anything to do with your spiritual life. Or, maybe you have. In either case, do that (again) by asking:

- What do I immediately think of when I encounter the word "delight"?

- Who or what has most nurtured and supported my sense of delight?

- Which aspects of faith and traditional spiritual practice do I associate with delight?

Consider the Alternatives	
Delight	
This . . .	*Or this . . .*
Gladdened	Anguished
Fascinated	Depressed
Jubilant	Grim
Overjoyed	Unhappy

SECTION III

Self-Care
on the Journey

Chapter 10

Spiritual Practice Burnout

Consider this scenario: Your night table is stacked with devotionals you've stopped reading. You'd prefer not to say when you last wrote in your prayer journal. Rather than greeting the day with formal Morning Prayer, you toss "hey, thanks" to the universe as you head toward coffee and computer. The rest of your day includes ignoring the calendar alerts you once dutifully set for mid-morning, midday, and mid-afternoon prayer. At the end of the day, you're already half-asleep before remembering to do a quick examination of conscience, so you mentally skip through it hoping everything gets worked out in your dreams.

And to think, you were once so devoted and disciplined and determined to master every single one of the traditional practices. You loved them! You loved the growth that became possible because of them. You did all things spiritual without too much ceasing. Now, months or years later, you're not only core level exhausted in body, mind, and spirit, but you can't quite muster enough enthusiasm to practice any of them. Oy verily, you cannot stomach them.

When it comes to traditional practices, your decline in interest could be due to the demands of everyday busyness or disaffection with ones that once worked for you (see Chapter 4: Sorting Through Structure). Another possibility: you're in the throes of burnout, and not from "refiner's fire," which is something else (Mal 3:2; 1 Pet 1:7). Resistance and fiery melt-down are predictable pit stops along the spiritual journey (see Chapter 1: About That Spiritual Journey). Try to find a saint's autobiography or memoir by a contemporary Seeker without at least one reference to, if not detailed description of, the "fire of transformation." But these are almost always descriptions of *spiritual awakening*, not *spiritual practice burnout*.

Spiritual awakening involves being temporarily overwhelmed by waves of emotions, heightened sensitivity to sensory input, sleep disorders and intense dreams, and a sense of disloca-tion—and that's when it's at the level of spiritual emergence rather than spiritual emergency. Spiritual emergency is when all this becomes intense enough to become an emotional and behavioral crisis, albeit not one necessarily requiring psychi-atric intervention. To underscore this distinction, "Religious or Spiritual Problem" was added to the DSM-IV[1] in 1994. The new DSM category distinguished mystical experiences from symptoms of impending or full-blown psychosis, emphasizing the non-pathological nature of mystical experience.[2]

To be super-clear, while there's obvious overlap when you look at the origins, spiritual flameout is not the same as spiri-tual practice burnout.

Burnout is the fatigue, apathy, and, in most cases, complete breakdown of body, mind, and spirit from overwork.[3] It was devel-oped by psychologists with reference to the world of occupations and professions. But since burnout stems from achievement-driven behavior, it's an appropriate way to label the negative con-sequences of working too long or too hard at (too many) spiritual practices, especially ones involving a lot of doing.

If the fruits of the spirit include but are not limited to love, joy, peace, patience, and faithfulness (Gal 5:22-23), then feeling exhausted and hopeless indicate an erosion of spirit, one that won't be alleviated by working harder to master spiritual practices. (This, unfortunately, can reach new heights of depths in spiritual communities when *ora* becomes indistinguishable from *labora*—and not in a healthy or balanced way.)

Are all enthusiastic Seekers at risk for burnout? Can't enthusiasm just be enthusiasm? Must an embrace of spiritual practices turn into a viselike grip? No, yes, and no.

Seekers most at risk for spiritual practice burnout are those who already tilt toward overachievement, have a history of linking achievement to self-worth, and don't live an especially balanced life to begin with. Staying longer at the office becomes sitting longer in meditation. Skipping meals to focus on work becomes skipping meals to focus on spiritual practice. Dismissing social gatherings as less important than work becomes viewing them as less valuable than spiritual practice.

You, perhaps? Me, for sure. If so, then surprise, no surprise—you've shifted attitudes and beliefs about the value of hard work to your spiritual practices. Here's what's predictable: whatever you do in your so-called everyday life, you will do in your spiritual life.

Is It Self-Preservation . . .

- You know the signs of spiritual practice burnout and address them in (almost) real time.
- You swiftly seek and follow counsel from experienced elders who have your best spiritual interests at heart.
- You consciously choose to take a break from practices and are flexible about returning to them.

. . . Or Is It Self-Sabotage?

- You view all signs of spiritual distress as exciting!
- You procrastinate about asking for counsel or help from experienced elders.
- You rely on your own instincts and best thinking about your spiritual practices and push through.

But wait! Seekers are committed to consciousness about whatever causes or perpetuates dis-integration, so how the holy ___ did *this* happen?

How could it not?

Belief in working hard to get ahead is woven into the fabric of life in Western culture. The work ethic is revealed by idioms about going the extra mile, making great strides, and stopping at nothing to achieve success.

You're especially at risk for defaulting to this achievement construct if doing more has helped you get ahead; achieving more helped you stay there. You're at risk if you were raised in a religious tradition where achievement is more or less linked to eligibility for salvation or proof of God's favor. Not you? Okay, then maybe you know someone?[4]

Alas, while being a longtime Seeker may slow this default behavior down long enough for you to notice and stop it, do not count on it happening automatically. This change in deeply grooved behavior will, paradoxically, take practice. But oh dear God, *not* more of what you've already been doing. Let's not go to the problem to fix the problem. Instead, to deal with burnout, try practicing:

- *Willingness:* Be willing to receive feedback from those who notice attitudinal and behavioral shifts they think might be due to overworking some/all spiritual practices. When someone suggests you might be heading for trouble, the correct response is, "Thanks, please tell me what you see" rather than "am not."

  Become willing to get a reality check and actively seek out guidance from an experienced teacher or spiritual director, especially if you tend to slog through everything on your own. Lack of guidance as well as lack of social support is more likely to turn spiritual emergence into a spiritual emergency.

- *Curiosity:* View changes in moods, behavior, and physical well-being as invitations to explore how these might be connected to the intensity of your spiritual practice. Learn how to do a Body Scan and use it to explore what you're feeling physically and where you're feeling it (see Appendix B).

- *Generosity:* Give yourself a generous break. You're not the first person whose enthusiasm for all things spiritual got a little—or a lot—dysfunctional. And on the subject of breaks, go ahead and take one or ditch a traditional practice entirely. For a while (see Chapter 12: Relaxation and Rest).

Igniting spiritual awareness and steadily feeding the flame of spiritual hunger is one thing. Self-immolation by spiritual flameout or spiritual practice burnout is something else. Neither will allow you to continue the journey without unnecessary suffering. Once again, twelve-step recovery offers this wise observation about transformation: "Pain is mandatory, suffering is optional."

Perhaps it's time to stop and reassess not where you're going but how you're getting there. These practices of being—willingness, curiosity, and generosity—will help you do exactly that and possibly more than you can imagine when you're in near-complete burnout.

> ### *Burnout: Spiritual Practice Version*
>
> Around 2006, psychologists Herbert J. Freudenberger and Gail North identified twelve phases of the (work) burnout process.[5] I've tweaked it to develop these sequential stages of spiritual practice burnout:
>
> 1. Enthusiasm for spiritual practices. ("I love how these practices boost my spiritual growth.")
> 2. Focusing on mastery. ("I want to do these practices better because that's . . . better.")
> 3. Practicing more frequently and rigorously. ("Practicing more rigorously will enhance my spiritual stature and standing among other Seekers.")
> 4. Neglecting "worldly" responsibilities and obligations. ("I'll get to bill paying/housework/yard work/food shopping after I finish praying/meditating/contemplating/soaking in Scripture.")
> 5. Spiritualizing negative moods. ("I'm suffering, so this must be working.")
> 6. Withdrawing from community. ("I need to stay focused on my practices.")
> 7. Feeling frustrated and cynical. ("Are these practices even working? I'm going and getting nowhere.")
> 8. Feeling apathetic. ("Why bother?")
> 9. Avoiding the practice—burnout. ("I'm exhausted.")

KNOW THYSELF—
SPIRITUAL PRACTICE BURNOUT

Spiritual practices! You've gone way beyond trying them all and now you're suffering unintended consequences. Relative to your practices, either something not good is happening or on the verge of happening. Examine your situation more closely by asking:

- How often do I assess my spiritual practice load (i.e., number of practices, frequency of practice)?

- What story am I telling myself (and others) about the importance of my current spiritual practices?

- How close to spiritual practice burnout am I getting?

Chapter 11

Solitude

"Be still, and know . . ."[1]

Superb idea but easier intended than done. Many times during your spiritual journey you've wanted to be alone yet resisted solitude. You were taught that sacred community is a sacred crucible for sacred growth, so you figured it would be too un-sacred to take a break from all that sacred. Perhaps you're also working a twelve-step program of recovery and have been repeatedly cautioned about the dangers of isolating and know it would be dangerous to put yourself in danger.

And yet, you find yourself wanting to get away from it all. Sometimes "it all" is the beloved community of Believers and Seekers. What was once spiritually energizing has become depleting. Other times "it all" are traditional practices. What was once spiritually illuminating has become dulled by overuse. Once you were found but now you feel lost. There's amazing grace in realizing that you need renewal and restoration.

Good news: you're not alone in periodically wanting—and needing—time alone. Extra good news: making time for solitude is considered a sign of spiritual maturity.

Every spiritual tradition encourages Seekers to set aside alone time during which external distractions and diversions are significantly reduced, if not eliminated entirely. Solitude is a sacred time-out entered into with intentionality to help deepen spiritual awareness and support spiritual growth.

You won't have to scroll too far through Scripture to find examples of going solo to facilitate meet-ups with the Almighty. God appears only after Jacob sends off his wives, servants, and sons (Gen 32:22-30). For Moses, face time with God, receiving Torah, and holy hissy fits happen during solitary trips up Mt. Sinai (e.g., Exod 19:3, 20, 23; 24:12-18). Moses holed up in the tent of meeting alone to receive yet more guidance from God about dealing with the tribes (Exod 19:5; 33:7-11). Elijah scores quality time with God after fleeing to a cave (1 Kgs 19:1-18). Solitude and stillness are exalted by the psalmist (Ps 46:10) and whoever wrote Lamentations points out, "It is good that one should wait quietly / for the salvation of the LORD" (Lam 3:26).[2]

Solitude is considered such an essential element of prayer that Jesus flat out tells followers to pray alone in their rooms and to do so behind closed doors (Matt 6:6). Also in red letters: stop with the overwrought public piety and blabbage (Matt 6:5, 7).

By that point in gospel accounts Jesus has already been sent to the desert by the Spirit for a forty-day vision quest and dust-up with Satan (Matt 4:1; Mark 1:12; Luke 4:1). And although they were written by different authors, at different points in history, and with different agendas, all four gospels recount substantively similar stories about Jesus opting for solitude. Jesus wanders off before dawn to solitary places (Mark 1:35, 45), withdraws to deserted places (Luke 5:15-16), seeks respite from miracle-hungry and somewhat handsy crowds by escaping in a boat (Matt 14:13) and going to a mountain (Matt 14:23; 15:29; Mark 6:46; Luke 6:12).

And you probably already know the basic, if not the more detailed, history of Western monasticism, yes?[3] The monastic tradition is where a core paradox of spiritual life is discovered and lived: communal solitude. Being alone together is a good and healthy thing for sacred spelunking because of the (mostly silent) support provided by community.[4]

The need for and ability to create solitude amidst community is a recurring theme in lives of the saints and spiritual teachers. Biographers of saints never fail to reference St. Catherine of Siena's "little interior oratory within her own soul" and "interior closet." Saint Francis de Sales underscores this in *Introduction to the Devout Life* with his own counsel to "make occasional retreats into the solitude of your heart, whilst outwardly engaged in business or conversation." Saint Teresa of Ávila provides a guided tour of the "interior castle." One of the twentieth century's most influential and well-known spiritual teachers, Thomas Merton, explains how true solitude doesn't come from external conditions but "is an abyss opening up in the center of your own soul."[5]

Truly you could spend a lifetime or a marvelous private retreat studying instructions for interior solitude. In any case, here's what twenty-first-century Seekers really need to know: Not only is solitude a venerable way to support spiritual growth, but it's an essential form of self-care. Be still, know God . . . and lower your blood pressure and restore:

- *Balance:* You're doing too much or feel as if you're doing too much, especially with others. Removing external pressures to participate will help reveal what's out of whack and mitigate impending spiritual practice burnout (see Chapter 10: Spiritual Practice Burnout).

- *Focus:* Your concentration is . . . squirrel! Removing interruptions and distractions will help reveal what's getting in the way of identifying what's important and paying attention to what is seen and unseen.

• *Creativity:* You're losing your ability to think deeply or differently. Removing the onslaught of information, input, and feedback will help enhance your ability to figure things out by yourself, although the divine is always present and providing input.

In the context of spiritual life, solitude, especially when coupled with silence, is a healthy choice. No need to worry about being too busy for solitude because even relatively brief periods of scheduled alone time can make a big difference in your attitude, outlook, and blood pressure level (i.e., lowering it). You can benefit from taking an afternoon walk or an extra-long bath. Try eating at least one meal alone every day without reading, watching television, or checking your smartphone. A full meal. Sitting at a table rather than looming before the refrigerator with a fork.

No need to worry about living in the secular world because there are plenty of ways to practice solitude without joining a monastery.[6] You can visit one! Or, you can mirror monastic conditions by observing designated periods of silence (see Chapter 12: Relaxation and Rest). You can create your very own vision quest at home, hopefully without a dustup with Satan.

Vision Quest: *Try This at Home*

Ah, the vision quest—an ancient rite of passage usually discussed in the context of Native American rituals, but which seems to have a broader cross-cultural and historical presence. Grossly simplified, the vision quest involves accessing divine guidance about identity and purpose by plunging into nature alone.

Fortunately, you do not have to banish yourself to a mountain or desert without food, water, or indoor plumbing. You can have a perfectly credible vision quest in the relative comfort of your own home by turning off the phone, suspending cable service, blocking Internet access, and committing to solitude for at least a weekend. Forgo coffee, chocolate, potato chips, and ice cream for the duration if you want a more ascetic experience, but all you need is an uninterrupted chunk of time without external stimulation.

And intentionality, commitment, and patience. Remember, this is not a staycation during which you repaint the laundry room.

Commit to being as quiet as possible, with senses wide open. At its core, the vision quest is about asking to be shown the truth of your life, then waiting for a message whose content and delivery you couldn't possibly predict in advance.

Note: Contraindicated for anyone who tends to turn solitude into isolating, or anyone with a history of clinical depression.

Any good reasons to be cautious about solitude? Not to be a bliss kill but the answer here is, "yes." Personality and other psychological factors are important considerations.

If you're an extrovert, solitude may end up draining rather than restoring energy. If, because of your extraordinarily active face-to-face or online social life you've developed a case of FoMO (Fear of Missing Out),[7] you should consider easing into solitude with very brief periods of solitude. Plunging into a weeklong silent retreat at a monastery could be shocking enough to undermine its purpose.

Conversely, if you're an introvert, you'll need to build in support so solitude doesn't devolve into social isolation. You should be able to return to community refreshed and restored after a period of solitude, not needing to be alone because being with others has become intolerable. Solitude heals and empowers because it's intentional and voluntary; social isolation is neither.

Is It Seeking Solitude . . .

- You consciously and happily choose to set aside time to be alone.
- You're excited about what will become possible during and because of your time alone.
- You know that a period of solitude will be refreshing, restorative, and sacred.

. . . Or Is It Isolating?

- You actively avoid contact with others so you can be alone.
- You'd rather be alone than feel awkward and out-of-sync with others.
- You often forget how lonely and depressed you feel when you're alone for too long.

If you've ever wrestled with depression, then communal solitude for a specified duration with accountability is the wiser, healthier choice. Solitude is not healthy self-care if you end up feeling lonely and disconnected while disguising it as piety.

Basically, the challenge is knowing when to take a sacred time-out and when to return to the land of the living, giving, and loving. Prepare for solitude by spending some time in discernment with experienced elders to help you figure out whether you're hoping for restoration or escape, practicing willingness to explore this possibility. Seek guidance about when, where, and for how long to schedule time alone.

Discerning Discernment

You may think that the word "discernment" refers to the ability to correctly assess a situation and, on the earth plane, you'd be right. Dictionaries define discernment as a skill of perception involving the senses or intellect. Seeing is believing and makes accurate distinctions possible.

Spiritual life changes the vectors between belief and sight. For Seekers, believing helps seeing more acutely and clearly what is often unseen. Discernment is defined as the ability to correctly identify the spiritual source of any call to action. For some with the "gift of knowledge," discernment is near-instantaneous and accurate. And then, there's everyone else.

Learning how to discern true from false, and then how to follow through, is yet another spiritual practice that takes practice. It also involves checking with spiritually mature others to ensure the "small still voice within" isn't just your own.

Depending on your personality and experience, kick off your solitude by announcing to the cosmos, "Here I am, now what?" Otherwise do a bit of planning about how you'll use this time. At the very not-so-least, plan to practice curiosity and delight about whatever emerges during your solitude and behold how self-care has become a spiritual practice.

Monastery Retreat 101

Challenge: Solitude. Solution: Monastery Retreat?

Seems like an obvious and wise solution, given how monastic life is anchored in the spiritual disciplines of solitude and silence. Still, keep in mind these three key factoids: (1) monastery life is community life; (2) unless you book yourself into a hermitage, you won't be totally alone; and (3) the flow of monastery life can be a bit of a jolt at first. Additional things to clarify as you plan a monastery retreat:

- *Goals:* Want a guided retreat? Prefer being completely on your own? Planning to focus on creative work (e.g., writing or art)?

- *Expectations:* Expecting complete silence over and beyond the Great Silence after Compline? Hoping to participate in community life (e.g., serving in the kitchen)? receive spiritual direction? take in beautiful scenery?
- *Special needs:* Need accommodations for food allergies or special diets? Require a physically accessible room? refrigeration for medications? a private room and/or bathroom?

Prepare for realities like, oh, incense. If you have inhalant allergies, inquire about its use and find a different monastery if this is an issue. You might be asked to surrender your smartphone and/or there may not be any WiFi connectivity. Could be a problem if you're planning to write and need access to online resources.

Pack earplugs if you're hypersensitive to noise because silence doesn't always equal quiet. Not keen on austere? Not a problem! There are plenty of monastic retreat centers with great food and gorgeous walking trails. Plus incense, chanting, a fabulous gift shop, and local massage therapists on call.

KNOW THYSELF—SOLITUDE

Now that you think more about it, you realize that spiritual seeking and even some of the traditional practices to support it can generate a lot of internal (and sometimes external) racing around. Set aside some alone time to explore all that by asking:

- When have I been most drawn to solitude? When has alone time seemed a disturbing prospect?

- What might become more available or possible if I set aside times for solitude?

- How do I need to rethink, restructure, and reschedule my sacred time alone?

Chapter 12

Relaxation and Rest

Hey, look at you remembering the Sabbath and keeping it holy. It's one of the Ten Commandments, so you're really working it.[1]

Sometimes you'll begin Sabbath at sundown on Friday and observe it until Masterpiece Theatre airs on PBS on Sunday evening. You bought a slow cooker so you won't have to toil in the kitchen. You stay home alone and study Scripture, as quiet and still as the un-resurrected dead. You keep your mortal flesh silent by shutting down online access, dumbing down your smartphone, and wearing industrial strength earplugs to block noise. And as a result, Sabbath rest isn't exactly restful, but at least you're doing it by the book . . . scroll . . . whatever.

Truth be revealed and told, you'd have an infinitely better chance of relaxing and resting on Wednesdays because that's when your work schedule can be cleared. Labor-intensive cooking methods felt marvelously meditative long before you ever heard of Brother Lawrence or read the contemporary classic-for-a-generation, *Chop Wood, Carry Water.*[2] Visits with friends are refreshing, especially when you select the friends and time frame. You're enriched by conversations via social media; inspired by Instagram images of nature and ones tagged #InstaPray, #seeGod, and #visualtheology. Physical exercise tops your list of tried-and-true ways to reduce stress and ensure quality sleep. The earplugs ended up blocking out soothing sounds of the sacred in birdsong, rain, crickets, exuberant frogs, and purring.

Seem familiar? If so, you're in good company with Seekers who never quite relax and rest because everything is always being worked on or worked out—spiritually, of course. These are the Seekers who take Christian Scripture exhortations about staying awake a bit too literally (e.g., Matt 24:42-43 and Mark 13:35-37; Mark 14:38).

They for sure and possibly you need to relax and rest. Relaxation and rest are essential forms of self-care for Seekers, whether the impetus for doing them comes from divine commandment, impending burnout from overzealous spiritual practicing, or demands of secular daily life.

To begin, you may need to revise some—or lots—of your current thinking about relaxation and rest, starting with the vectors. Instead of thinking "rest and relaxation" when you see R&R promotions (especially by retreat centers), think: "Relaxation and Rest." Physically and psychologically speaking, relaxation (i.e., physical unwinding, mental and emotional release) leads to rest (i.e., restorative sleep, refreshing inactivity, emotional serenity)—not the other way around.

Give this an empirical whirl by attempting a nap (i.e., brief period of sleep) while feeling hypervigilant, thinking about everything you absolutely must do, and experiencing tachycardia. Notice how much more easily you can surrender into deep sleep (i.e., suspended sensory and voluntary muscle activity) after relaxing with a brisk walk and/or warm bath. Notice the relaxing relief of silence after a full day talking, especially if your day job involves teaching and preaching, consulting, counseling, and coaching. Sing in a choir or the shower and then notice how rest comes easier after giving your respiratory system a workout.

Next, you may need to examine cultural assumptions and personal fears about how relaxation and rest—especially yours—might be perceived as:

- *Laziness*: Are you concerned that setting aside time to stop working is really just (sinful) laziness on your part?

- *Unavailability*: Do you worry about being perceived as unavailable and stingy in spirit?

- *Frivolous:* Have you been raised to believe that having fun is not only trivial, but evidence of superficiality?

- *Boring:* Has the adrenaline rush of hyperactivity, chaos, and noise (external and internal) made serenity seem undesirably dull?

Well? Any of this going on for you in general? How about when you think about giving some or all traditional spiritual practices a rest? Here again, these practices of being—willingness, curiosity, and generosity—will help you discover what might be undermining your self-care (see Chapter 10: Spiritual Practice Burnout).

Is It Resting . . .

- You welcome stillness and quiet as an opportunity to take a break from thinking and planning.
- You exercise, cook, garden, and spend time with friends to relax.
- You easily drift from napping to deep dreamless sleep.

. . . Or Is It Waiting?

- You welcome stillness and quiet as an opportunity to think about the future.
- You exercise, cook, garden, and spend time with friends to work off energy.
- You have difficulty napping and your sleep is a jumble of disturbing dreams.

Having explored all this, but oh dear God *not* during your Sabbath, you'll be better equipped to make smart choices about times to keep silence and times to speak (Eccl 3:7); times for "a little sleep, a little slumber, / a little folding of the hands to rest" (Prov 6:10).

Fascinatin' Biorhythms

According to Western medicine, changes in physical, mental, and behavioral health follow a 24-hour cycle.[3] These cycles, known as circadian rhythms, are affected by body temperature, light, and the interrelationship of heart rate, blood pressure, and hormone levels.

To be fair, founders of monastic orders knew nothing about this, nor were they able to control light to the extent that we're now able, when they established schedules for prayer, study, and work. Ditto for when the Divine Office/Liturgy of the Hours/Canonical Hours were developed.

According to Western medicine, optimal wake-up time is between 6:00 and 7:00 a.m. Major mental activity should be scheduled to happen between 8:00 a.m. and noon when body temperature is elevated. The largest meal of the day should be scarfed down (or meditatively eaten) between noon and 3:00 p.m., with a nap scheduled in there as well. Rising body temperature between 3:00 and 4:00 p.m. makes that a good time for another round of mental activity. Physical exercise is most effective at the end of the day when motor skills are high and muscles are already warmed up.

Optimal time for the deep sleep needed for physical repair and mental restoration is between 1:00 and 5:00 in the morning, so getting to bed by midnight makes sense.

Now, let's be fair to you. Depending on how closely your personal biorhythms align with normative circadian rhythms, strict adherence to a traditional schedule for prayer practice may be more than merely disruptive and could become life-threatening.

Knowing now that relaxation precedes rest, learn how to use proven physical self-care techniques to relax muscles, such as Progressive Muscle Relaxation (PMR)[4] and/or Body Scan Meditation, a form of Vipassana (Buddhist) meditation popular among practitioners trained in the Mindfulness-Based Stress Reduction (MBSR) developed by Jon Kabat-Zinn during the late 1970s.[5] Learn how to breathe more fully and deeply by studying with a teacher who is specifically knowledgeable, trained, and experienced in *pranayama* (yogic breathing).[6] After acknowledging that circadian rhythms are a thing, re-examine and reschedule the times you've set aside for relaxation (especially exercise) and rest (especially napping and sleeping). Find ways to exercise without making it a blood sport.

Learn and use self-care techniques known to release mental obsessions and reduce anxiety, such as ones taught by therapists trained and experienced in Cognitive Behavioral Therapy (CBT). While you're at it, tidy up the room or rooms where you plan to rest because agitation can be triggered by visual as well as auditory noise, an insight from Feng Shui 101.[7]

Restore fun and therefore relaxation to games by playing without keeping score. And since relaxation does not mean inactivity, you might want to choose among activities you already experience as relaxing and add new ones to your options (e.g., cooking, gardening, arts and crafts, coloring, jigsaw puzzles).

Trend Alert: Coloring Books for Adults

ICYMI,[8] coloring books for adults have recently reemerged as a gateway to relaxation and fun. That's right, reemerged because more than ninety years ago, psychoanalyst (and spiritual Seeker) Carl Jung prescribed coloring to patients. Jung, who sketched a mandala (Sanskrit: circle) each morning, recommended coloring these intricate geometric patterns to support psychological integration and balance.

Current advocates of coloring books for adults laud how coloring is relaxing, enhances focus and concentration, boosts self-confidence about art, and helps both sides of the brain work together. Detractors include art therapists who are not keen on using preconceived designs. Some spiritual teachers draw a thick wobbly line between meditation and meditative-like activities.

Advocates and critics do agree that coloring books are fun, relaxing, and harmless. They could add "spiritual," because the most popular coloring books seem to be ones featuring mandalas. So there.

Have faith that you can do profound and deep spiritual work without feeling like a pack animal, which, by the way, are also commanded by the Almighty to get some Sabbath rest (Deut 5:14).[9] But really, you don't have to be well-versed in either Hebrew or Christian Scripture to know that Sabbath observance is about taking a break from work. You might, however, need to remember that work isn't only physical but also cognitive, behavioral, and yes, spiritual.

You'll definitely need to explore if, how, and when the spiritual disciplines you've practiced during times of rest have become work or worse, drudgery. Might be time to relax your grip and give them a rest, but you may not be able to do that until you get some yourself. Go forth, relax, and let the rest happen.

Into Great Silence: Try This at Home

The Carthusian Order of hermit monks have lived in solitude and silence since 1064.[10] Monks and nuns in almost all other monastic orders do not, in fact, take a "vow of silence," but promise to maintain an "atmosphere of silence" but may speak as necessary (e.g., true emergencies, structured community dialogue, spiritual direction) or on special occasions. Typically, a system of hand signals develops to facilitate communication.

All monastics observe the Great Silence (i.e., no talking; a.k.a., Grand Silence, *magnum silencium*) between the close of Compline (i.e., approximately 9:00 p.m.) and Prime (i.e., approximately 6:00 a.m.). Go ahead, try this at home, eliminating television, radio, music, or podcasts as well as talking to enhance the silence.

Before including additional periods of silence during your day:

- contemplate your reasons and goals for this;
- think through when and for how long your silence will last;

> - decide if and how to use nonverbal forms of communication; and
> - alert others in advance so you don't come across as rude or hostile.

KNOW THYSELF—RELAXATION AND REST

You know full well that you're supposed to be resting and others have told you to chillax, but what does that even mean? What does it mean to relax and rest in the context of spiritual life when it's supposed to be about getting and staying awake, and embracing practices that help you do that? Take a closer look at your attitudes and behaviors by asking:

- What have I been taught or told about resting and relaxing?

- Why might my preferences for relaxation and rest not look like that to an observer?

- When and how do I realize that relaxation and rest is probably a good idea?

Appendix A

Cheat Sheet

The Practices of Being in Three Simple but Not-so-Easy Steps

Having trouble remembering how to do these practices of being? After first delighting in that irony, use the following key action words to help support your practice.

Practical options: copy these onto an index card that you'll keep handy, and/or onto a physical or digital sticky note to post where you're most likely to notice.

Willingness
1. Allow
2. Accept
3. Surrender

Curiosity
1. Wonder
2. Explore
3. Discover

Empathy
1. Experience
2. Feel
3. Share

Generosity
1. Acknowledge
2. Appreciate
3. Give

Delight
1. Encounter
2. Recognize
3. Generate

Appendix B

Spiritual Survival Skills

The Body Scan

While your mind is busy figuring stuff out, your body knows exactly what's going on, sometimes physically manifesting things like doubt, fear, and aggravation. Our cultural recognition of body wisdom is captured in such phrases as "a pain in the neck," "digging in your heels," "shouldering burdens," and "being pissed off."

The body-mind connection will come as no news if you've practiced yoga or worked with a therapist trained to recognize body-mind connectivity issues, but how well do you understand it? You could also read mountains of materials that explain the body-mind connection in great esoteric detail, but committing to doing a regular Body Scan will be a more efficient, instructive, and useful way to develop conscious awareness about this connection.

Here's how to do a Body Scan:

- *Find a quiet place and time*, until you get to the point where you can quickly scan your body under any and

105

all conditions and circumstances. Close your eyes to block out visual distractions. Take a few deep breaths to settle down and into what you're doing.

- *While either sitting, standing, or lying down, use your "mind's eye" to mentally scan your body.* You can start scanning from any direction—head to feet, feet to head, from belly out to extremities. It doesn't matter where you begin the scan, just begin it.

- *As you scan, notice what you're feeling in the most literal sense.* What feels tingly, sore, numb, heavy, large, achy, constricted, open, tight, warm, cold? Does one side have more sensation than the other? The entire side or just part of it? What happens when you draw an imaginary line dividing the front of your body from the back, top from bottom, head from body? Are your extremities attached to your torso, or do they feel disembodied? Feeling nothing? Notice that because feeling "nothing" is still feeling. Notice how feeling blank differs from feeling numb.

- *Do not get caught up in attaching value labels to what you feel.* Your sense that something is bad, wrong, or good indicates that your mind's eye is wandering around your brain.

- *Put your scan on pause whenever you feel discomfort.* Pause so you can really feel what's there physically. Is it discomfort or pain? Are you feeling the sensations or trying to figure out where they're from or what they mean? Stay focused on physical sensations without trying to figure anything out. Paradoxically, not focusing on meaning will probably reveal it, although generally not at that precise moment.

Note: While this may seem similar to the Body Scan Meditation taught by Mindfulness practitioners, the goal of this Body Scan is different. Here, the point is to cultivate awareness of how your body physically manifests emotions, no shortage of which will emerge during spiritual practices. The goal of the Body Scan Meditation is relaxation and . . . mindfulness.

Appendix C

Your Rule of Spiritual Life

The Rule of St. Benedict isn't the only rule ever created to guide spiritual life in a monastic setting, but it's probably the best known. The Rule works for many reasons, but mostly because of its emphasis on balance. Neither prayer nor study nor work dominate daily existence. All activities—not just prayer—are seen as sacred. The Rule ensures that these activities are rotated throughout the day and night, while also encouraging times for renewal (a.k.a., recreation) and hospitality (i.e., service).

And, the Rule provides a useful model for creating personal guidelines for your spiritual life.

Even if you don't want to formalize an individual rule, exploring the questions below will help:

- reveal where and how you experience the sacred;

- disclose what helps you stay awake and aware;

- provide a reality check about what does or doesn't support your spiritual growth; and

- identify your spiritual priorities for daily life.

Note: These questions will take time and focus to answer, so don't even think of slamming through them in one sitting. Don't work on them when you're supposed to be relaxing and resting. And for the love of all that's sacred, do *not* work on them at all if doing so will interfere with your practices of being.

Spiritual Practices and Activities

- Which ones have best supported my spiritual awareness?

- Which ones have best supported my spiritual growth?

- Which ones do I always return to even after taking a break?

- Which ones help me experience the sacred in daily life?

- Which ones are already a regular feature of my daily life?

- Which ones do I observe (pretty much) weekly?

- Which ones have I wanted to ditch?

What would help ensure that my spiritual life is intentional?

Structural Issues

- What forms of structure support my spiritual growth?

- Which forms of structure seem to impede my spiritual growth?

- How do I currently fit/integrate spiritual practices into daily life relative to:
  - family?
  - work?

- friendships?
- the community-at-large?
- To what extent does the liturgical calendar help organize my spiritual life?
- To what extent do Lectionary readings help organize my spiritual life?

What would help ensure that my spiritual life is balanced?

Cognitive, Emotional, and Behavioral Issues

- How do my learning style and cognitive abilities affect my spiritual life?
- Which practices seem to support my emotional well-being?
- Which practices tend to disturb my emotional well-being?
- How do I actively care for my cognitive, emotional, and behavioral health?
- How do I typically measure spiritual growth?
- How do I define "spiritual results"?
- How important is it for me to measure and mark spiritual growth?

What would help ensure that my spiritual life is healthy?

Support Issues

- Who is in my current network of support for spiritual life?
- Do I currently work with a spiritual director?

- Do I currently work with a psychotherapist?

- Do I currently work with a life coach?

- (If in twelve-step recovery) Do I currently work with a sponsor?

- How do I know when I need support for my spiritual life?

- When do I tend to resist support for my spiritual life?

What would help ensure that my spiritual life is supported?

$\mathcal{N}$otes

Chapter 1: About That Spiritual Journey

1. Although the terms are often used interchangeably, emoticons and emojis are different ways to express emotions in online text. Emojis are actual pictures (i.e., pictographs), while emoticons use type to convey facial expressions. Here, for example, is the most common way to represent eye rolling: @@. I'm also fond of this emoticon: :-P For more geekery, read Jeff Blagdon, "How emoji conquered the world: The story of the smiley face from the man who invented it," *The Verge*, March 4, 2013, http://bit.ly/1NgfZmI.

2. See Tom W. Smith, "Spiritual and Religious Transformations in America: The National Spiritual Transformation Study," National Opinion Research Center/University of Chicago, December 9, 2005, http://bit.ly/1O3fwq9. See also Arthur J. Schwartz, "The Nature of Spiritual Transformation: A Review of the Literature," Fall 2000 http://bit .ly/1Nwo45O.

3. One of my all-time favorite prayers from the Hindu tradition: "From the unreal lead me to the real! From darkness lead me to light! From death lead me to immortality!" Found in George Appleton, ed., *The Oxford Book of Prayer* (New York: Oxford University Press, 1985), 282.

4. In use among academicians for nearly 20 years and added to the *Oxford English Dictionary* in 2015, cisgender refers to people for whom sex status at birth is aligned with gender identity. See Paula Blank, "Will 'Cisgender' Survive?," *The Atlantic*, September 24, 2014, http://theatln .tc/207sqau.

5. See, for example, Holly Nelson-Becker and M. Carlean Gilbert, "Spirituality and Older Women: The Journey Home to Self," Loyola University Chicago School of Social Work: Faculty Publications and Other Works, Paper 33, 2014, http://bit.ly/1NwBMFJ.

6. Lars Tornstam, "Maturing into Gerotranscendence," *The Journal of Transpersonal Psychology* 43, no. 2 (2011): 166–80, http://bit.ly/1NwXFot. Tornstam, *Gerotranscendence: A Developmental Theory of Positive Aging* (New York: Springer, 2005).

Chapter 2: About Those Spiritual Practices

1. Any of mine? No joke, I spent much of the 1990s writing about this stuff for magazines like *Natural Health*, *Holistic Living*, and *Vegetarian Times*, which were keen on reviving venerable spiritual practices long before Emergents emerged. I'm inordinately proud of having had some of this work reprinted by *Utne Reader*. Never heard of *Utne Reader*? Don't tell me, I don't need additional signs of aging.

2. For what is perhaps the most frequently cited typology for spiritual practices, see Richard J. Foster, *Celebration of Discipline: The Path to Spiritual Growth* (New York: HarperOne, 1978, 1988, 1998). Foster defines and sorts spiritual practices into the Inward, Outward, and Corporate Disciplines. For another relatively recent crack at this, see Brian McLaren, *Finding Our Way Again: The Return of the Ancient Practices* (Nashville, TN: Thomas Nelson, 2008).

3. Conversations about being "spiritual but not religious" began as early as 2001 with Robert C. Fuller's book *Spiritual, But Not Religious: Understanding Unchurched America* (New York: Oxford University Press, 2001). These discussions picked up momentum nearly a decade later with the LifeWay Research project (Rob Phillips, "Research: Millennials Are Spiritually Diverse," 2010, http://www.lifeway.com/Article /LifeWay-Research-finds-American-millennials-are-spiritually-diverse) and the Pew Forum on Religion and Public Life ("Religion Among the Millennials," 2010, http://www.pewforum.org/files/2010/02/millennials -report.pdf). Social science data, so it must be true!

4. Alcoholics Anonymous World Services, *Alcoholics Anonymous*, 4th ed. (New York, 2001), 568.

5. Between 2009 and 2012, I prayed (mostly Compline) from the Daily Office on Twitter with @virtual_abbey. This online community began in 2009 when author, scientist, and then-abbess of The Urban

Abbey, Raima Larter, decided to tweet Morning Prayer as her Lenten discipline.

During Lent 2012, our community decided to go on hiatus to reassess our mission and structure. By then, we had a prayer team of six people taking turns tweeting Matins and Compline, as well as an occasional Sext and Vespers. Read more about the process by visiting http://bit.ly/zWwHZN.

As of July 2015, @virtual_abbey had racked up 72.7K tweets, 6,271 followers from around the world, and many more who attended prayer without officially following the Twitter account. I know this because I was elected the really virtual abbess in 2010 and helped lead the hiatus discernment process in 2012.

6. Painting an icon? Not writing an icon? What?!? American iconographer Fr. Peter Pearson takes on this (and other controversies) in his books, *A Brush with God: An Icon Workbook* (Harrisburg, PA: Morehouse, 2005) and *Another Brush with God: Further Conversations about Icons* (Harrisburg, PA: Morehouse, 2009). With his characteristic wit and wisdom, Pearson points out linguistic differences between ancient Greek and contemporary English to explain why he prefers "painting" rather than "writing" icons (64–65).

7. Note: that's "aural" as in auditory not energy auras. Don't believe in energy auras? Clearly you need to meet more mystics.

8. I believe learning styles have extraordinary explanatory value, but you already know this because you've read my previous work, right? For the importance of understanding learning styles relative to using online social networking platforms, see *The Social Media Gospel: Sharing the Good News in New Ways*, 2nd ed. (Collegeville, MN: Liturgical Press, 2015).

9. Thanks to what I fondly refer to as The Yoga Years, I'm most familiar with Patanjali's Eight Limbs of Yoga. Patanjali, who lived in the second century BCE or fifth century CE, codified spiritual disciplines practiced in the Eastern hemisphere as early as 3000 BCE. The Eightfold Path of Yoga involves practicing: (1) Yama (ethical rules/social contracts); (2) Niyama (inner disciplines/daily observances); (3) Asana (physical posture); (4) Pranayama (breath control); (5) Pratyahara (drawing attention inward); (6) Dharana (concentration on one point/image); (7) Dhyana (meditation without an object); (8) Samadhi (pure contemplation).

10. This sentence seem familiar? If you're reading this book then I'm guessing you have a refrigerator magnet with this quote from Mahatma Gandhi: "You must be the change you wish to see in the world."

Chapter 3: Powerful Paradox

1. Wisdom from Carl Jung: "Oddly enough, the paradox is one of our most valuable spiritual possessions, while uniformity of meaning is a sign of Weakness. Hence, a religion becomes inwardly impoverished when it loses or waters down its paradoxes; but their multiplication enriches because only the paradox comes anywhere near to comprehending the fullness of life. Non-ambiguity and non-contradiction are one-sided, and thus, not suited to express the incomprehensible" (C. G. Jung, *Psychology and Alchemy*, vol. 12 in *The Collected Works*, trans. R. F. C. Hull).

2. Zen Buddhist practice includes meditating on *koans* (paradoxes), believing that enlightenment is attained and possibly in a split-second, once reason is completely abandoned. I'm going to resist snarky speculation about the half-life of that enlightenment for the average Western-turned-Eastern meditator.

3. Pierre Teilhard de Chardin, "Trust in the Slow Work of God," turned into a prayer/poem (http://bit.ly/1e1zCkm), originally appeared in a letter de Chardin wrote in 1915. *The Making of a Mind: Letters from a Soldier-Priest, 1914–1919* (New York: Harper & Row, 1965).

4. Rant Alert: Mystery is not the same thing as magic, which involves producing illusions. Still, there's no shortage of magical thinking among good people of faith who attribute causality to actions (or lack thereof). I'm thinking here about how teachings about generosity have gotten twisted up in a personal reward system, which then gets defended by claiming the power of witness: Look what God did for me! God can do that for you, too! Get rich! And not just symbolically! (See Chapter 8: Generosity.)

5. Thanks to the popularity of Neuro-Linguistic Programming (NLP) during the 1970s and 1980s, reframing became more widely known as a technique. It was, however, used as early as the 1940s by psychiatrists Milton H. Erickson, MD, and Viktor Frankl, MD.

Chapter 4: Sorting Through Structure

1. Best quote from the movie "Ghostbusters," delivered by Bill Murray in the role of psychologist Dr. Peter Venkman: http://bit.ly/1Ib4GZx.

2. News Flash from Soc. 101: Social institutions are not the same as what are colloquially known as "total institutions" such as the military, mental hospitals, prisons, and monasteries. Social institutions are norms, values, statuses, roles, and expectations that develop from and stabilize basic social needs. Total institutions, a term developed by

Erving Goffman, are formal organizations that re-form and reassign social status, role, and identity by cutting members off from the rest of society. Erving Goffman, "On the Characteristics of Total Institutions," presented in April 1957 at the Walter Reed Institute's Symposium on Preventive and Social Psychiatry. Reprinted in Goffman, *Asylums: Essays on the Social Situation of Mental Patients and Other Inmates* (Garden City, NY: Anchor Books, 1961). You can read and download a PDF of the essay here: http://bit.ly/1Ib8ZEd.

3. Here, I believe, would be an excellent place to note that Phyllis Tickle, of blessed memory, characterized religion as "the schizophrenic first cousin of faith" in her book *God-Talk in America* (New York: Crossroad, 1997), 174. The sentence in which that appears continues to note how religion "is less and less a part of god-talk these days and more and more a part of cerebral talk—a conversational element in the planning of the good society, the living of the good life, the creation and nurture of the good family."

4. Shameless Self-Promotion Alert: For more about my Jewish upbringing and the durability thereof, read, *Why Is There a Menorah on the Altar?: Jewish Roots of Christian Worship* (New York: Seabury Books, 2009), http://amzn.to/16zGGzl.

5. For more information about the United States' "religious landscape" in general, see "Religious Landscape Study" from Pew Research: http://pewrsr.ch/1IbarGJ. For more information about "Christian Movements and Denominations," see: http://pewrsr.ch/1IbaIJQ and "Appendix B: Classification of Protestant Denominations," http://pewrsr.ch/1IbaUIQ. These are data as of May 2015. Knowing what I know about denominational dustups, there could be a few more denominations by the time this book gets published.

6. For an Anglican take on this, see this 2011 piece by Rev. Dr. Patrick Malloy, PhD, made available online by the Episcopal Diocese of New York. Note especially this view: "The rubrics are the 'ground rules' that the Church has put in place to insure that both the rights and duties of all the members are honored. . . . the rubrics are not dictatorial but democratic, and are not controlling but liberating" (http://conta.cc/1Ibd0IW).

7. Yes, I made this up. You're welcome.

8. The psalmist sings, "Bless the Lord at all times" (Ps 34:1). Meanwhile, the Abrahamic religions have structured prayer like this:

Judaism—Three Daily Prayers: (1) Shacharit (morning); (2) Mincha (afternoon); and (3) Arvit/Maariv (evening). Christianity—Eight Daily Prayers (Liturgy of the Hours/Divine Office): (1) Matins/Vigils/Nocturns (midnight); (2) Lauds (dawn or 3:00 a.m.); (3) Prime (early morning or ~ 6:00 a.m.); (4) Terce (mid-morning or ~ 9:00 a.m.); (5) Sext (midday or noon); (6) None (mid-afternoon or ~ 3:00 p.m.); (7) Vespers (evening or ~ 6:00 p.m.); and (8) Compline (night or ~ 9:00 p.m.). Islam—Five Daily Prayers: (1) Fajr (pre-dawn); (2) Dhuhr (midday): (3) Asr (afternoon); (4) Maghrib (sunset); and (5) Isha'a (night). Friday Prayer (replaces Dhuhr).

9. This is as good a place as any to recall this wisdom from the rooms of twelve-step recovery: "Religion is for people who are afraid they'll go to hell. Spirituality is for people who have been there."

10. See "Understanding Obsessive-Compulsive and Related Disorders," Stanford School of Medicine, http://stanford.io/1TaxZQV. Need /want more science? Read LR Baxter Jr, ME Phelps, JC Mazziotta, BH Guze, JM Schwartz, CE Selin, "Local cerebral glucose metabolic rates in obsessive-compulsive disorder. A comparison with rates in unipolar depression and in normal controls," *Arch Gen Psychiatry* 44, no. 3 (March 1987): 211–18, http://1.usa.gov/1TaymLf.

Chapter 5: Willingness

1. This is it, my one and only reference to anything by Mary Oliver. "The Summer Day," from *New and Selected Poems* (Boston, MA: Beacon Press, 1992).

2. Wags in AA quip that denial is an acronym for: **D**on't **E**ven **N**otice **I** **A**m **L**ying.

3. "Toddler refusal," a stage in the process of developing self-awareness and becoming a separate self (i.e., individuation). It's essential for establishing and maintaining healthy boundaries later on in life.

4. By the time I reached my 50s, I'd already logged decades of therapy in many different therapeutic modalities, with male as well as female therapists. If we ever meet in person, do feel free to ask me about my adventures. For now, I just want to brag about the time I found someone trained in CBT (Cognitive Behavioral Therapy), plus savvy about Bowen Family Systems Theory and Imago Relationship Therapy who also had experience with clergy families. #Win

5. Yes, I chose forty days on purpose, because of its significance in Hebrew and Christian Scripture and holy day/season observance.

6. See Chapter 4: Sorting Through Structure for a brief description of the Examen. Possibly my favorite introduction to the Examen is this lovely little book by Jim Manney, *A Simple, Life-Changing Prayer: Discovering the Power of St. Ignatius Loyola's Examen* (Chicago: Loyola Press, 2011).

7. I claim bragging rights to being able to locate many of these references within the Big Book *Alcoholics Anonymous* and *Twelve Steps and Twelve Traditions*, but not all. To find all of them, I searched through the online version of *164 and More*, a concordance for these basic texts for twelve-step recovery: www.164andmore.com. Who rocks the Internet? Me! Who isn't at all humble about that skill? Me!

Chapter 6: Curiosity

1. When it comes to viewing curiosity as a spiritual practice, I'm in very good company. In her book *Sacred Pause: A Creative Retreat for the Word-weary Christian* (Brewster, MA: Paraclete Press, 2014), Rachel G. Hackenberg articulates what I've long believed: "Fostering such [child-like] curiosity within ourselves is a necessary spiritual practice. It is the willingness to know how much we don't know . . . and simultaneously to believe far more than we deem certain or 'factual.' Curiosity must be nurtured, personally and interpersonally, in order for faith and for faith-in-community to grow" (134).

2. Why do we yawn? While it seems as if it has to do with being tired, that's apparently only because exhaustion increases brain temperature. Rather than a mechanism for getting more oxygen to the brain, yawning is a way to cool it down. See http://bit.ly/1K62vF0. For a more entertaining read, see Maria Konnikova, "The Surprising Science of Yawning," *The New Yorker*, April 14, 2014, http://nyr.kr/1K62DUQ. Also, note: Brian K. Rundle, Vanessa R. Vaughn, Matthew S. Stanford, "Contagious yawning and psychopathy," *Personality and Individual Differences*, November 2015, http://bit.ly/1HTTLA7.

Chapter 7: Empathy

1. For the next time game night includes Trivial Pursuit: the word "empathy" was introduced by British psychologist Edward B. Titchener in 1909 because it was easier to remember and pronounce than *Einfühlung* (German: "feeling into"), which German philosopher Rudolf Lotze coined in 1858 as a substitute for ἐμπάθεια (*empátheia*) (Greek:

passion). For excruciating detail about this linguistic development, read "Empathy" in Stanford Encyclopedia of Philosophy, revised, February 14, 2013, http://stanford.io/1gN53QE. For a much-abbreviated etymology, see this entry at the Online Etymology Dictionary: http://bit.ly/1gN5Ktr.

2. Metta (a.k.a., loving-kindness) meditation involves silently or quietly repeating four short resolves or wishes, starting with self before extending to categories of others both known and unknown, liked and disliked. The traditional sequence is:

May [I and then others] be free from danger.
May [I and then others] have mental happiness.
May [I and then others] have physical happiness.
May [I and then others] have ease of well-being.

Larger and more inclusive categories are invoked until the practitioner is ready to end with:

May all beings without exception be free from danger.
May all beings without exception have mental happiness.
May all beings without exception have physical happiness.
May all beings without exception have ease of well-being.

For variations with less formal language, type "metta meditation" into your browser's search bar.

3. For one of the more complete lists of feeling states, emotional and physical, see "Feelings Inventory," The Center for Nonviolent Communication, http://bit.ly/1L0oD6X. For the all-time best cartoon about the pain scale chart with faces, see Allie Brosh, "Boyfriend Doesn't Have Ebola. Probably," Hyperbole and a Half, February 10, 2010, http://bit.ly/HRRDxA.

4. John Gray, *What You Feel, You Can Heal* (Mill Valley, CA: Heart Publishing, 1994).

5. For examples of interdisciplinary programs that combine wisdom from social scientists and neuroscientists, see the Greater Good Science Center at the University of California, Berkeley, http://bit.ly/1TH93Pl; The Center for Compassion and Altruism Research and Education at the Stanford School of Medicine, http://stanford.io/1NjtsKz; Cognitively-Based Compassion Training (CBCT) at Emory University, http://bit.ly/1NjtRg9; Center for Compassion Studies at University of Arizona, http://bit.ly/1NjufLw.

6. On YouTube, see Brené Brown on Empathy: http://bit.ly/1ZkUjLI.

7. Internet slang for intense feelings, "feels" first arrived on the scene in 2010, became an Urban Dictionary entry on March 30, 2012, and took

off in October of that year when it was posted to Facebook as a meme. The hashtag #allthefeels shows up regularly on social media, providing a great example of how "saying it don't make it so."

8. Developed in 1990 by psychologists John Mayer and Peter Salovey, the theory of emotional intelligence was reworked and introduced to the general audience by Daniel Goleman in *Emotional Intelligence* (New York, NY: Bantam Books, 1995). Even earlier, psychologist Howard Gardner included "Interpersonal Intelligence" (i.e., perception of other people's feelings) within his seven-type model when he introduced Multiple Intelligence Theory in *Frames of Mind* (New York, NY: Basic Books: 1983).

9. For evidence-based tips for teaching empathy to children plus references to research, see Gwen Dewar, "Teaching empathy: Evidence-based tips for fostering empathy in children," Parenting Science, January 2014, http://bit.ly/1TGzox5. The landmark observation that empathy "can't be taught but can be caught" is in Mary Gordon, *Roots of Empathy: Changing the World, Child by Child* (Toronto: Thomas Allen, 2005).

10. Can't resist taking more-than-a-peek at these debates? Knock yourself out, but don't get too distracted by conversations about whether "poverty simulations" can instill empathy and lead to more compassion; see S. Y. Nickols and R. B. Nielsen, "'So many people are struggling': Developing social empathy through a poverty simulation," *Journal of Poverty* 15, no. 1 (2011): 22–42, http://bit.ly/1TGufVC. Or, this heated debate about empathy and public policy sparked by Paul Bloom's article, "The Baby in the Well: The case against empathy," *The New Yorker*, May 20, 2013, http://nyr.kr/1Na9Rxi; plus this Forum piece, "Against Empathy," *Boston Review*, September 10, 2014, http://bit.ly/1Naa43x; and the poop storm about it on Reddit: http://bit.ly/1NaaarP; as well as this more recent opinion piece by Daryl Cameron, Michael Inzlicht, and William A. Cunningham, "Empathy Is Actually a Choice," *The New York Times*, July 10, 2015, http://nyti.ms/1Na9pze. If you do opt to plow through this stuff, then be assured of my deepest empathy, which comes from having spent more than a decade in academia.

11. John Welwood, "Principles of Inner Work: Psychological and Spiritual," *The Journal of Transpersonal Psychology* 16, no. 1 (1984): 63–73, http://bit.ly/1MgrHcz. For even more, visit www.johnwelwood .com/bibliography.htm.

12. Robert Augustus Masters, *Spiritual Bypassing: When Spirituality Disconnects Us from What Really Matters* (Berkeley: North Atlantic Books, 2010). For an excerpt, see http://bit.ly/1PS4EL3.

13. AA cofounder Bill Wilson on the gift of suffering: "Suffering is no longer a menace to be evaded at any cost. When it does come, no matter how grievously, we realize that it too has its purpose. It is our great teacher because it reveals our defects and so pushes us forward into the paths of progress. The pain of drinking did just this for us. And so can any other pain" (Editorial, *AA Grapevine*, November 1958).

14. For more information and resources, see www.compassionfatigue .org.

15. Empathy Quotient (EQ) questionnaire developed by Simon Baron-Cohen: http://bit.ly/1j6o82h. For an overview of current empathy measurements, see Karsten Stueber, "Empathy," *The Stanford Encyclopedia of Philosophy*, Winter 2014 Edition, ed. Edward N. Zalta, http://stanford.io/1iTXIjw. For a table of empathy questionnaires, see http://bit.ly/1iU4h5B.

16. Interpersonal Reactivity Index (IRI) developed by Mark H. Davis: http://bit.ly/1j6qDS4. Also, Davis, "A Multidimensional Approach to Individual Differences in Empathy," http://bit.ly/1iU1Yzv.

17. Reading the Mind in the Eyes test developed by Simon Baron-Cohen: http://bit.ly/1j6sBls.

18. Self-Compassion Test developed by Kristin Neff: http://bit.ly /1j6riD7.

19. Ken Dychtwald, *Bodymind* (Los Angeles: Tarcher Putnam, 1986) is the classic (very readable) text.

Chapter 8: Generosity

1.These days, Christian faith communities define tithing as setting aside 10 percent of income and paying it to the church to disburse among those in need. Although tithing is viewed as a moral and ethical obligation, the consequences of *not* tithing varies by church community. Net income? Gross income? Categories not specified because they didn't even exist at the time, something that gives us yet another thing to argue about, usually without noticing the legalistic irony of doing so.

2. Try writing out a list of things/people/situations for which you are grateful. Start off with a reasonable number of items. If you set out to enumerate some insane number like 50, you'll end up including stuff that not even the most zealous gratitude junkie would list. Better to limit yourself to three good reasons to be grateful than to end up complaining about having to dredge up sludge from a too-deep well.

3. When it comes to financial generosity, watch out for overcorrecting. While you probably can easily fork over 10 percent and possibly more of your income, giving to the point of becoming financially unstable is foolishness, arrogance, or both.

4. One version of "The Prayer of St. Francis" reads like this:

Lord, make me an instrument of thy peace.
Where there is hatred, let me sow love;
Where there is injury, pardon;
Where there is doubt, faith;
Where there is despair, hope;
Where there is darkness, light;
Where there is sadness, joy.

O divine Master, grant that I may not so much seek
To be consoled as to console,
To be understood as to understand,
To be loved as to love;
For it is in giving that we receive;
It is in pardoning that we are pardoned;
It is in dying to self that we are born to eternal life.

The one that shows up in twelve-step recovery literature reads like this:

Lord, make me a channel of thy peace—
that where there is hatred, I may bring love—
that where there is wrong, I may bring the spirit of forgiveness—
that where there is discord, I may bring harmony—
that where there is error, I may bring truth—
that where there is doubt, I may bring faith—
that where there is despair, I may bring hope—
that where there are shadows, I may bring light—
that where there is sadness, I may bring joy.
Lord, grant that I may seek rather to comfort than to be comforted—
to understand, than to be understood—
to love, than to be loved.
For it is by self-forgetting that one finds.
It is by forgiving that one is forgiven.
It is by dying that one awakens to Eternal Life.
(Alcoholics Anonymous World Services, *Twelve Steps and Twelve Traditions* [New York, 2002], step 11, p. 99).

Neither version was written by St. Francis, but appeared circa 1915 (see http://bit.ly/1ihOsG4). Also, the Easter Bunny isn't real and Rosebud was a sled.

5. Another goodie from the rooms of twelve-step recovery: "Healing begins when the blaming ends."

Chapter 9: Delight

1. #SeeWhatIDidThere

2. Shout-out to Rev. Laurie Ferguson, PhD, for mentioning "attention with intention" during yet another wonderful phone call. Need a personal coach or consultant with a track record of working with leadership? I recommend her: http://lauriejferguson.com/.

3. For those keeping count at home, this from Daniel L. Aiken, "Delight," www.biblestudytools.com: "The idea of delight occurs approximately 110 times in Scripture in various forms. Less than fifteen occurrences are found in the New Testament. The related concept of 'please' occurs about 350 times, about seventy-five of these occurrences in the New Testament."

4. Appointed Feasts of the Lord, as established in Leviticus 23: Sabbath, Passover and feast of Unleavened Bread, feast of First Fruits/feast of Weeks (Shavuot), feast of Trumpets (Rosh Hashanah), Day of Atonement (Yom Kippur), feast of Tabernacles (Sukkot). Rejoice in the Law (Simchat Torah), which is observed the day after Sukkot is completed, celebrates receiving the Law of Moses (Torah: Genesis, Exodus, Leviticus, Numbers, Deuteronomy). In Hebrew, *simcha* means gladness or joy.

5. Note how Abraham's laughter upon getting this news flash from God is more incredulous and derisive than it is delighted (Gen 17:17).

6. Norman Cousins, *Anatomy of an Illness as Perceived by the Patient: Reflections on Healing and Regeneration* (New York: W.W. Norton, 1979).

7. For comprehensive overviews of this research, see William B. Strean, "Laughter prescription," *Canadian Family Physician* 55, no. 10 (2009): 965–67, http://1.usa.gov/1Mjh8Ww; and Ramon Mora-Ripoll, "The therapeutic value of laughter in medicine," *Alternative Therapies in Health and Medicine* 16, no. 6 (2010): 55–64, http://bit.ly/1MjiFf3.

8. After all these years, still one of the best books about the women mystic saints: Carol Lee Flinders, *Enduring Grace: Living Portraits of Seven Women Mystics* (San Francisco: HarperSanFrancisco, 1993).

9. You can probably quote at least the first line of this poem by Gerard Manley Hopkins, SJ (1844–89): "The world is charged with the grandeur of God" (http://bit.ly/1hESnvn). How about the one from E. E. Cummings (1894–1962) that begins: "i thank You God for most this amazing day . . ." (http://bit.ly/1hESx60 [linked to a YouTube video of Cummings reading his poem]).

10. Attributed to Pierre Teilhard de Chardin, SJ (1881–1955).

11. "The Family Afterward," in Big Book, *Alcoholics Anonymous*, 4th ed. (New York, 2001), 133.

12. Andrea Tornielli, "Pope Francis: the fifteen 'diseases' of the Curia," *Vatican Insider*, December 22, 2014, http://bit.ly/1va6VCR. "It is the disease of people who are 'scowling and unfriendly and think that, in order to be serious, they must show a melancholic and strict face and treat others—especially those, whom they think are inferior—with rigidity, harshness and arrogance.' In reality, adds the Pope, 'theatrical strictness and sterile pessimism are often symptoms of fear and insecurity about themselves. The apostle must strive to be a polite, serene, enthusiastic and joyful person . . .'"

13. Addiction and recovery experts distinguish substance-based addictions (e.g., alcohol, drugs, nicotine) from behavioral-based or "process" addictions (e.g., love, sex, gambling, shopping). Common to all addictions is the death grip that either the substance or the process (or both!) has on the person. See Meredith Gould, *Staying Sober: Tips for Working a Twelve Step Program of Recovery* (Center City, MN: Hazelden, 1999).

14. Wait, what . . . funerals? Yes, in the Christian tradition especially, funerals are intended to be a celebration of life and the joy of going home to God: Rest in peace, rise in glory! For a whole lot more about traditions for celebrations, see Meredith Gould, *The Catholic Home: Celebrations and Traditions for Holidays, Feast Days, and Every Day* (New York: Image/Doubleday, 2004).

15. Kate Torgovnick May, "5 new technologies that help disabled and bedridden people experience the world again," TEDBlog, May 7, 2015, http://bit.ly/1VT5Hz7. See also Virtual Photo Walks (VPW): http://bit

.ly/1VT5vjp. Also check Instagram for accounts with extraordinary photos of nature and travel; see Cole Mellino, "7 Instagram Accounts Every Nature Lover Should Be Following," EcoWatch, August 4, 2015, http://bit.ly/1hF795e. One of my IG faves for a glimpse of the Divine: usinterior.

16. Enduring great resources for working through blocks to imagination and creativity include Roger von Oech, *A Whack on the Side of the Head* (New York: Warner Books, 1983); von Oech, *A Kick in the Seat of the Pants* (New York: Harper and Row, 1986); and Julia Cameron, *The Artist's Way: A Spiritual Path to Higher Creativity* (New York: Jeremy P. Tarcher/Putnam, 1992).

Chapter 10: Spiritual Practice Burnout

1. The DSM, used by mental health professionals to code conditions primarily for billing purposes, is currently in its fifth edition. A code for "Religious or Spiritual Problem" (V62.89/Z65.8) was added to DSM-IV thanks, in part, to work by Stanislav and Christina Grof's identification and definition of "spiritual emergency," as well as work by David Lukoff in the mid-1990s. For more about this history, see Darlene B. Viggiano and Stanley Krippner, "The Grofs' Model of Spiritual Emergency in Retrospect: Has it Stood the Test of Time?," *International Journal of Transpersonal Studies* 29, no. 1 (2010): 118–27, http://bit.ly/1OSvQZ7. This journal article also includes references to essential readings about spiritual emergency.

Also, please watch and listen to this video by Lukoff, in which he talks about the background for the DSM category: http://bit.ly/1NnQO0h. Also, visit and tour through the Spiritual Competency Resource Center: http://www.spiritualcompetency.com/.

2. David Lukoff, "The diagnosis of mystical experiences with psychotic features," *The Journal of Transpersonal Psychology* 17, no. 2 (1985): 155–81, http://bit.ly/1OSzu5p.

3. For one of the better articles about burnout for a general audience, viz., without any fancy-pants technical language, see Sherrie Bourg Carter, "The Tell Tale Signs of Burnout . . . Do You Have Them?," *Psychology Today*, November 26, 2013, http://bit.ly/1KiN77u.

4. Look at that, I just wrote in upspeak!

5. Twelve phases of the burnout process developed by psychologists Herbert J. Freudenberger and Gail North, discussed in Ulrich Kraft, "Burned Out," *Scientific American Mind* (June/July 2006): 28–33.

Chapter 11: Solitude

1. Psalm 46:10. Has anyone ever written about solitude without quoting this psalm verse? Doubtful and I, for sure, am not going to be the first.

2. Was the nameless author of Lamentations really the prophet Jeremiah? If you were raised Christian, you probably think it was, thanks to St. Jerome, who translated Scripture into Latin during the fourth century CE, but consider this Jewish perspective: Naftali Silberberg, "When Was the Book of Lamentations Written?," Chabad.org, http://bit.ly/1MwjerX.

3. FWIW, I believe that basic knowledge of Western monasticism, as developed by St. Benedict of Nursia during the sixth century CE, includes knowing about its Eastern Orthodox roots starting with Desert Fathers (late third century CE) and Desert Mothers (fourth and fifth centuries CE). Somewhat more esoteric basic knowledge would include knowing distinctions among ways solitude has been practiced within community (e.g., cenobites) and somewhat attached to community (e.g., hermits, anchorites).

4. For a comprehensive look at contemporary community, see Robert D. Putnam, *Bowling Alone: The Collapse and Revival of American Community* (New York: Touchstone, 2001). For a critique about how digital technology has led to being "alone together" but not in a good way, see Sherry Turkle, *Alone Together: Why We Expect More from Technology and Less from Each Other* (New York: Basic Books, 2011). For critiques of Turkle's critique enter "Turkle is wrong" into the search engine.

5. Thomas Merton, *New Seeds of Contemplation* (New York: New Directions, 1972), 80.

6. Here's one primer: Brother Benet Tvedten, *How to Be a Monastic and Not Leave Your Day Job* (Brewster, MA: Paraclete Press, 2006).

7. Fear of Missing Out Quiz: http://www.ratemyfomo.com/.

Chapter 12: Relaxation and Rest

1. Extra religious education points for you if you know that the numbering differs among Christian denominations and between Jews and Christians. This is exactly the type of esoterica I simultaneously love and loathe. Jews and most Protestants rank "Remember the Sabbath day by keeping it holy" as commandment #4, right after the one about messing with the Lord's name (#3) and before the commandment to honor parents (#5). Catholics and many Lutherans rank keeping the Sabbath as the #3 commandment by blending what everyone else considers #1 and #2.

It still ends up appearing after the commandment about not dissing God and swearing (#2) and before the one about honoring parents (#4).

2. Another big must-read hit from the golden age of self-discovery and personal growth during the mid-1980s through late 1990s: Rick Fields, *Chop Wood, Carry Water: A Guide to Finding Spiritual Fulfillment in Everyday Life* (New York: Jeremy P. Tarcher, 1984). Rediscovered during the late 1960s: Brother Lawrence, *The Practice of the Presence of God* (Grand Rapids, MI: Spire Books, 1967). In Jana Riess's must-read book about spiritual practices, *Flunking Sainthood: A Year of Breaking the Sabbath, Forgetting to Pray, and Still Loving My Neighbor* (Brewster, MA: Paraclete Press, 2011), chapter 3: "meeting Jesus in the kitchen . . . or not."

3. India's 5,000-year-old system of medicine, Ayurveda, and Traditional Chinese Medicine (TCM), which has been practiced for more than 3,000 years, identify different times as optimal for sleeping, eating, exercise, and concentration. When it comes to sleep, Ayurvedic practitioners recommend getting to sleep by 10:00 p.m. and TCM practitioners suggest doing so no later than 10:30 p.m.

4. See, for example, these downloadable PDFs: Progressive Muscle Relaxation (PMR): http://bit.ly/1GQ7qyO and http://bit.ly/1XWmOO2. Search YouTube for videos, if you'd prefer audiovisual guidance, or Spotify if you prefer just audio. In either case, preview these to make sure the voice of the person guiding PMR doesn't irritate you.

5. See "What is Mindfulness-Based Stress Reduction?" at Mindful Living Programs: http://bit.ly/1XWnqn1. Also, Center for Mindfulness in Medicine, Health Care, and Society at the University of Massachusetts Medical School: http://bit.ly/1GQ8na6, the program developed by Kabat-Zinn. For an example of the body scan used during Mindfulness-Based Stress Reduction (MBSR) see http://bit.ly/1XWneny.

6. To learn more about this yogic practice, read all linked articles at "Beginner's Guide to Pranayama," *Yoga Journal*, October 10, 2014, http://bit.ly/1XWnVxi. Take it from me, this is a form of breath work that should be learned live and in person from a live and in person teacher. You've been warned!

7. Feng shui is the ancient Asian art of arranging all the crap you have in your home or office so you don't freak out, plunge into poverty, or get physically sick from bad vibes. It has been around for 4,000 years and combines science, intuition, mysticism, astrology, sacred geometry,

and common sense. In China and Japan, feng shui masters are routinely included on architecture, building, and interior design teams. Still, that hasn't stopped some Western observers from freaking out about feng shui. If that includes you, just stop reading this footnote and go back to the text. Maybe also consider sitting elsewhere to read.

8. ICYMI = In Case You Missed It, in case you missed that. How meta, right?

9. "But the seventh day is a sabbath to the LORD your God; you shall not do any work—you, or your son or your daughter, or your male or female slave, or your ox or your donkey, or any of your livestock, or the resident alien in your towns, so that your male and female slave may rest as well as you" (Deut 5:14).

10. For a felt experience of monastic silence, watch Philip Gröning's 2005 documentary about the Carthusian monks of the Grande Chartreuse monastery, *Into Great Silence*. All 162 minutes of it . . . without taking a break or eating popcorn.

Subject Index

Scripture Index